By Lillian Hellman

Plays

Memoirs

Editor of

PENTIMENTO

PENTIMENTO

A Book of Portraits

by Lillian Hellman

LITTLE, BROWN AND COMPANY · BOSTON · TORONTO

SECOND PRINTING

T09/73

Portions of this book originally appeared in *The Atlantic, Esquire*
and the *New York Review of Books.*

Library of Congress Cataloging in Publication Data

Hellman, Lillian, 1905-
    Pentimento.

    1. Hellman, Lillian, 1905-   I. Title.
PS3515.E343Z498   812'.5'2 [B]   73-7747
ISBN 0-316-35520-8

*Published simultaneously in Canada
by Little, Brown & Company (Canada) Limited*

PRINTED IN THE UNITED STATES OF AMERICA

For Peter Feibleman

Contents

PENTIMENTO

OLD paint on canvas, as it ages, sometimes becomes transparent. When that happens it is possible, in some pictures, to see the original lines: a tree will show through a woman's dress, a child makes way for a dog, a large boat is no longer on an open sea. That is called pentimento because the painter "repented," changed his mind. Perhaps it would be as well to say that the old conception, replaced by a later choice, is a way of seeing and then seeing again.

That is all I mean about the people in this book. The paint has aged now and I wanted to see what was there for me once, what is there for me now.

BETHE

THE letter said, says now, in Gothic script, "Bethe will be sailing between November 3rd and November 6th, the Captain of the ship cannot be certain. Be assured, dear Bernard, that we have full trust in intentions you have been kind enough to give to us. Her mother has put aside the pain in knowledge that nothing is here with us for her but a poor life. We have two letters from the Bowmans, Ernest and Carl Senior, assuring us that the arrangement will not be 'forced upon, etc.' and we know that yourself will make the final approval only if the young people should wish joinment. Bethe is well favored, as the sister you remember, some say even more. How strange the name New Orleans sounds to us, in the Southern States of America. As if our daughter is to travel to the lands of the Indies, we think it no less far. But nightly we say prayer that we will live to cross the sea, all our families to meet again."

The letter is blurred and the pages are torn in the folds, but the name Bowman appears several times and it is still possible to make out a sentence in which the writer tells of having sold something to make the voyage possible.

Bethe for a short time lived in the modest house on Prytania Street, sleeping on a cot in the dining room, rising at five o'clock to carry it to the back porch, to be the first to heat the water, to make the coffee, to roll and bake the German breakfast rolls that nobody liked. Then, to save the carfare, she walked the long distance to the end of Canal Street, where she carried shoe box stacks back and forth all day for the German merchant who ran a mean store for sailors off the wharves.

Two or three months after she arrived — there had been, through those months, a few short visits to whichever lesser Bowman was not too busy or too bored — she was taken to one of the great Bowman houses and there, finally, was introduced to Styrie Bowman, the husband planned for her in the long-distance arrangement. Many years later, when people had given Styrie up for dead, I was told that a journalist wrote a book about the period. Bethe entered the book for a reason she did not know on the day she met Styrie. I do not know the book or the journalist's name, but there is a cutting from the book pasted in a family album. "This same Bethe Bruno Koshland married Styrie Bowman, who was cousin to the powerful New Orleans cotton merchants. Styrie came and went so often and so far that it is impossible to trace his years between the time he was twenty and forty. He was described by many as having powerful force with women and yet all reports say that he was about five feet six, one side of his face an earth brown, and of almost fiend-like distortion. But like many ugly men he had success with women. The last traces of him occur in the home of Mrs. Finch of Denver, who supported him in style."

I do not know who Mrs. Finch was. In fact, I never knew much about Styrie, except the bare accounts, told to me so many years later, of the marriage that was arranged between him and Bethe. The Bowmans had been looking for someone who could clean up Styrie, keep him out of the hands of gamblers — there were too many forged checks that bore their names — and nothing better could be found than sensible, handsome, hardworking Bethe, who was also a third cousin and therefore to be trusted.

Two thousand dollars was raised by the Bowmans, a decent sum in those days for young people to begin a life, and a job was found for Styrie in a Bowman warehouse in Monroe, Louisiana. I never heard anybody say what Bethe felt about Styrie or the marriage, but certainly Styrie's feelings were clear, because six months after the marriage he disappeared, and Bethe returned to New Orleans. I remember breakfast talk about all that, and somewhere in those years I knew that Bethe was acting as governess — or whatever word the Bowmans had learned from their fellow Northern industrialists to call those who cared for their children — to one of the less important — less important meant less money — Bowman families.

I know all that I have written here, or I know it the way I remember it, which, of course, may not be the whole truth, because my grandfather was the Bernard of the letter sent from Germany and it was with his family that Bethe slept in the dining room and rose early to make the coffee. I am, therefore, a distant cousin to the Bowmans, but the only time they have ever acknowledged me was once, in a London hotel, when the Queen Mother Bowman complained to the manager that I played a phonograph in the apartment above her head.

Bethe arrived in New Orleans long before I was born, long before my father was married, but my grandfather and my father were great letter writers, competitive in what was then called a "beautiful hand." My father had little style — perhaps because he was so busy with the formation of the alphabet into shaded curls — but my grandfather, who had a few undergraduate years at Heidelberg, made charming, original observations in his letters and in the children's copybooks he used to make bookkeeping-household entries on one side of the page, and comments and memories and family jokes on the facing page. What isn't blurred, or isn't in code, is good to read: his memories of the Civil War — he became a quartermaster general of the Confederate Army in Florida, a job that pleased him because of its safety — oddly phrased comments on New Orleans, his children, his friends, his self-mocking comic attempts to become as rich as his cousins, the Bowmans. Many of these copy-books and letters — he evidently made a copy of every letter he wrote — were lost before I was born, but a surprising number of them remained by the time I first saw them, when I was sixteen, and I remember my pleasure in them, particularly the ingenious mathe-matical puzzles that he invented for himself and his friends.

That year, the year I was sixteen, Jenny, my fa-ther's sister, sold the boardinghouse she had owned for so many years and she and her sister Hannah moved to a small half-house that could not accommo-date the massive furniture, the old family portraits, the music and the books of their long dead father, much of which had come so many years before from Germany. For a few days I made myself useful to my aunts, but then the debris of other lives, the broken stickpins and cameos and ostrich feathers and care-fully wrapped pieces of exquisite embroidery, pleased me so much that I was allowed to carry them to the back porch and sit with them for days on end. This puzzled my aunts, who like all sensitive older people were convinced that youth had no interest in what it sprang from and so were careful not to bore the young with their own fancies or regrets. (I am now at the same age myself and the interest of students in my past has bewildered me and taken me too long to understand.)

My father's family, more than most, I think, did not speak of the past, although, if pressed, they had loving and funny stories of their mother and father. But I never knew, for example, until that time of their moving from one house to another that they had lost a brother in a yellow fever epidemic twenty years before I was born. I think the three of them, my father and my two aunts, had a true distaste for unhappiness, and that was one of the reasons I found them so attractive. In any case, it was on that porch, that sixteenth year of my life, that I discovered my grandfather's letters and notebooks and asked if I could have them for my own. Jenny and Hannah seemed pleased about that and for weeks after interrupted each other with amused, affectionate stories of my grandfather's "culture," his "eccentricities." When I returned to my mother and father in New York, I carried with me a valise with the letters and notebooks.

I suppose all women living together take on what we think of as male and female roles, but my aunts had made a rather puzzling mix-about. Jenny, who was the prettier, the softer in face and manner, had assumed a confidence she didn't have, and had taken on, demanded, I think, the practical, less pleasant duties. Hannah, who had once upon a time been more intelligent than Jenny, had somewhere given over, and although she held the official job, a very good one in those days of underpaid ladies, of secretary to the president of a large corporation, it was Jenny who called the tunes for their life together. I don't think this change-about of roles ever fooled my father, or that he paid much attention to it, but then he had grown up with them and knew about whatever it was that happened to their lives.

And so it was Jenny who wrote before my visit of the following year, asking me to bring back the letters and the notebooks of my grandfather. That seemed to me odd, but I put it down to some kind of legality that grown people fussed with, and carried them back. Perhaps I told them, perhaps I didn't, I don't remember, that during the year I had them, I had copied out some of them for what I called my "writer's book," a collection of mishmash, the youthful beginnings of a girl who hoped to write, who knew that observation was necessary, but who didn't know what observation was. All I really remember was the return of the valise and my conviction that it would come back to me when my aunts died.

Jenny died twenty years later. Hannah, lonely, bewildered, uncomplaining, lived on for another seven years, and one of the pleasant memories of my life is a visit that Dashiell Hammett made with me to see her. She was waiting for me at the New Orleans airport. She had never met Hammett and I had not told her he was coming with me. I was nervous because I knew she had never, could never approve a relationship outside marriage. As I came toward her, old now, the powerful body sagging, the strong face finally come into its own, outside the judgments of youth, the open, great smile faded as she realized that the tall figure behind me was Hammett and that she would finally have to face what she had heard about for many years.

The first day was a strain, but since Hammett was not a man to acknowledge such strains, the week's visit turned into a series of fine, gay dinners that worried Hannah at first by their extravagance, but came to please her when she realized that Hammett didn't even understand her protests. More important, all my father's family liked jokes, good or bad, and when Hammett, on the second day, told Hannah that all he had ever wanted in the world was a docile woman but, instead, had come out with me, the cost of the dinner at Galatoire's ceased to worry her, and she said that she, too, liked docile women in theory, but never liked them when she met them, and didn't he think they were often ninnies with oatmeal in the head. He said yes, he thought just that, but ninnies were easier women to be unfaithful to. She laughed at that and told me on our walk the next day that she thought Hammett was an intelligent man.

A year later I had a telephone call from a doctor I didn't know to say that Hannah was in the hospital. I went to New Orleans immediately to find a quiet, frightened old woman who had never been really sick in her life, and certainly never in a hospital. At the end of the week she seemed better and I made arrangements to go home, sure that she would recover.

(I have gone through my life sure that the people I love will recover, and if, in three cases, I have been wrong, at least I did them no harm and maybe curtained from them the front face of death.) I had, during that week, gone several times to her house to bring underwear or other things that Hannah needed in the hospital and I had seen the valise I had brought back so many years before. It was tied with the same cord I had put on it then, with the same red mark I had scratched on its side. It was standing in a closet next to a portrait of my grandfather and some old photographs, and I remembered that I had seen Jenny put it just there the day that I returned it.

But Hannah did not recover. She died a few days after I left New Orleans and I went back to give away the sad, proud, ugly things of her house. (She had left a will, giving me everything she had, more savings than I could have guessed from the deprived life she and Jenny had led.) Daisy, a Negro woman, who had come once a week for many years to clean the house for my aunts, brought her son and nephew, and as they hauled away the furniture to sell or keep or give away, we spoke about my aunts and what they would have liked me to keep for them. I decided to take a chocolate pot that had once belonged to my mother, my grandfather's portrait, family photographs, all the broken pieces of antique jewelry that had been piled in a tin box, a box of letters I had never seen before and, of course, the valise. But the valise was not to be found.

But I had seen it ten or twelve days before and

Daisy said she had seen it after that. A few hours later we found Hannah's door keys hidden in a flower-pot on the porch. Daisy said that was a habit of my aunts and it meant that somebody had been given the keys and told where to leave them when they were finished. Finished with what, Daisy asked me, but we both knew immediately that Hannah had given instructions to somebody to remove the valise. What friend, most of them too old or infirm to do such an errand? And why? Perhaps, I told myself, the last act of a private life. Or was it suspicion of me, a different breed, a writer, and therefore a stranger? But I had already seen the contents of the valise many years before and so that made no sense. On the plane going back to New York, thinking about it as the only alien, unfriendly act of Hannah's life, I remembered I had never read all that was there and when asked to return the valise I had told my aunts that and protested its return on that ground.

I don't know when in the next few years I came to believe that Bethe and Styrie and Mr. Arneggio had to do with the disappearance of the valise. When I thought about that, forcing myself into sleepless nights, knowing my memory is always best when I am tired, I pictured again old newspaper clippings and at least one long letter from Bethe in a German I couldn't read.

I am all out of order here — as most memories are — and even when I read my own childhood diaries, the notes about Bethe make no pattern, or they make a pattern in terms of years and seasons. But I cannot separate now what I heard described from what I saw or heard for myself.

I first remember Bethe, a tall, handsome woman in her late thirties, come to call on my aunts, always on a Sunday afternoon, carrying a large box of bad candy. Yes, her health was good, her small job was good, no, her coat was not too thin for the sharp damp of New Orleans winters, she had seen a good movie last Sunday and had a good Italian meal in a good Italian place for little money. I suppose it was the constant use of the word good, without a smile, that caused my mother, who was not to be predicted, to say to Bethe on one of the visits, "What a bitter life," and then leave the room with her hand over her eyes.

Bethe never stayed long on those occasional visits and would leave immediately when she was asked to eat supper with us, shaking everybody's hand and mumbling words that I often couldn't understand. Her accent was not German, but some strange, invented mixture as if she had taught herself English without ever hearing anybody speak it.

My aunts felt guilty about her, remembering their father's commitment, but my father would grow bored with their guilt and say that Bethe was a good-looking clod — he once said that she looked like him — and that he didn't believe Styrie's desertion had caused her anything more than a guttural sound in the throat. Jenny didn't like such talk, answering always that women were injured by the loss of husbands, no mat-

17

ter what stinkers, which is why she had never wanted one, and Mr. Crespie, one of my aunt's boarders, a former great lover of the town, would say that he had never thought much of Styrie, God knows, but that any man could be forgiven for leaving a German donkey like Bethe. I liked that kind of talk: I was coming to the age when I wanted to know what attracted men and what didn't; I would have liked to ask Bethe why men thought she was an unattractive clod, a donkey, when I thought her so handsome.

We were in New York when Bethe disappeared from her job with the Bowmans, because I remember Jenny telephoned my father to report it, and to ask him what she should do. He said that if everybody was lucky maybe Bethe had found a job in a nice whorehouse, and I heard Jenny's cackling laugh at the other end of the phone. But we were in New Orleans when Styrie reappeared, came to inquire for Bethe at my aunt's boardinghouse — I was miserable that I had been out at the time — and two days later was found beaten up somewhere along Bayou Sara. The good side of his face, I was told by Carl Bowman, Junior, older than I by a few years, wasn't good anymore, and the word Mafia came into Carl's talk, but I had never heard it before and it therefore meant nothing to me. I know Styrie stayed around New Orleans for a few months after that because Mr. Crespie said he saw him with some people in fancy clothes at a bar on Lake Pontchartrain. And then, suddenly, he was in the hospital.

Something must have worried the Bowmans — they were well known for shrugging off people who did not succeed — because Styrie had a private room and a night watchman was moved from one of the family warehouses to stand guard outside the room. But on the second night the room was shot up by two men in doctors' coats. When it was all over, Styrie was found clinging to a fire escape with his right hand because his left hand was lying on the ground.

I was allowed to stay home that day from school, and toward night I heard that the Bowmans had found Bethe in "a strange neighborhood," but that she had refused to visit her husband, using more sounds than words, finally writing in German that a visit from her might bring him further harm.

Perhaps nobody understood or perhaps the Bowmans were so sure of Styrie's imminent death that they felt anything was worth a respectable farewell. The two elderly Bowman uncles who escorted Bethe to the hospital told my father that Bethe seemed to "change" as she stepped into Styrie's room, because she "demanded" to be left alone with him. They said she came out mumbling in her "low-class syllables," shook hands with them, and disappeared before the two old fellows could find out where she was to be found for the funeral.

But there wasn't to be any funeral because that night the fevered, amputated Styrie disappeared from the hospital — the night watchman from the Bowman warehouse had a doped glass of Coca-Cola in his hand when they brought him around — and appears only once again, ten or twelve years later, in a letter from Mrs. Finch of Denver, reporting his death to Ernest, president of all the Bowmans, and asking for a memento or a photograph to remember him by. I know that caused a good deal of laughter in our house but Carl Bowman, Junior, my friend, said it caused anger in his.

It was a few years after Styrie's disappearance from the hospital — I was about thirteen, I think — that I was sent to Enrico's in the Wop section near Esplanade to buy oyster loaves for my aunts and me because on Sunday nights no dinner was served in the boardinghouse. I always looked forward to these suppers with my aunts, doors closed, jokes flying, Jenny singing after supper in a pleasant voice, regretting the opera that didn't come to town anymore, imitating her old music teachers.

I had chosen to go early for my walk on that pleasant spring night and have a good look at all the foreigners of the section around Enrico's. It was a conviction of my girlhood that only foreigners were interesting, had the only secrets, the only answers. A movie theatre — even now I can see the poster of Theda Bara, although I have no memory of the picture — was breaking between shows as I paused to examine Miss Bara's face, deciding to come back the next day for the movie. Then I saw Bethe. I started to call her name, never finished the sound, because she was with two men, a large, heavy man, and a young boy of about fifteen. When I did call her name, they were crossing the street and could not have heard me. I began to run toward them, but three oyster loaves, or the running time, or some warning, slowed me down and I came to follow so far behind that when they were a block ahead of me I lost them as they disappeared into a corner store. I took a streetcar home.

I don't know why I didn't tell my aunts that I had seen Bethe, but the next day I decided to skip school. I did this so often that my teachers, puzzled, in any case, by a girl who was shuttled between a school in New York for half the year and a New Orleans school for the other half, had ceased to care whether I showed up. I went immediately to the corner store. I walked around it for a long time until I saw two children go in. I followed them, having stopped to examine the window, full of sausages and cheese, canned goods and cheap candy boxes, and came into an empty store that had only two sausages hanging from the ceiling and one sparse shelf of canned stuff. And the children were not in the store. I waited for a long time and then tried a few soft hellos. When nobody came, I went out the door, rang a bell on the outside, and went back in to face the young boy I had seen in front of the movie.

I said, "I'd like a can of sardines, please."

When there was no answer, I said, "I like Italian sardines best. My father doesn't, he only likes the French ones. How much are they, please?"

21

The boy said, without accent, "We don't speak English here."

I said, knowing that many people in New Orleans liked only to speak the patois, "*Excusez-moi. Les sardines. Combien pour la boîte de sardines?*"

The boy said, "We have no cans of sardines."

"Yes, you have, I see them. Do you know my cousin Bethe?"

There was a sudden sound behind the door, and voices. The boy said, "Go, please, go out."

"That's not a nice way to talk. I wanted only to say hello to my cousin Bethe — " and stopped because I heard a man's voice; and then Bethe appeared in the door, turned to look at somebody I couldn't see, put up her hand, and shook her head at the young boy.

I said, "Good morning, Bethe, I'm — "

She said, very loudly, "How you find me here, *Liebchen?*"

"I saw you at the movies yesterday and I just wanted to say hello."

"Your family send you to this place?"

"No, no. I didn't tell them I saw you. I'm skipping school today, and I'd catch hell if they knew. What's the matter, Bethe, have I done wrong, are you mad with me?"

She smiled, shook her head, and turned to whoever was behind the door. She said something in a language I didn't know about and was answered. She listened carefully to the man's voice and said to me,

"No longer am I German. No longer the Bowmans. Now I am woman and woman does not need help."

She was smiling and I realized I'd never seen her smile before, never before heard her use so many words. But, more important to me, something was happening that I didn't understand. Years later I knew I had felt jealous that moment of that day, and whenever I have been jealous something goes wrong with my face. I guess it was going wrong then, because she said, "Do not sadden, *Liebchen*," and took my hand. She called out something cheerful to the man behind the door and we went for a walk.

We walked a long way, down toward the river, into streets and alleys I had never seen before. I don't remember her asking questions, but I told her about the books I was reading, Dickens and Balzac, about my beloved friend Julia in New York, and a joke about my mother's Uncle Jake and his money, and how bad it was to live without my old nurse Sophronia. As we waited for the streetcar that would take me home, I said, "Please, Bethe. I will never tell my family. I promise. I didn't come to see you for any reason at all except just coming."

But the words fell away and I knew that wasn't the truth. I was on my religious truth kick, having sworn on the steps of St. Louis Cathedral, and then in front of Temple Beth Israel, that I would never again in all my life tell a lie under threat of guillotine or torture. (God help all children as they move into a time of life they do not understand and must struggle through with precepts they have picked from the garbage cans of older people, clinging with the passion of the lost to odds and ends that will mess them up for all time, or hating the trash so much they will waste their future on the hatred.) And so sitting on that bench with Bethe waiting for a streetcar, I went into an incoherent out-loud communication with myself, a habit people complain about to this day, trying to tell her what was the truth in what I had just said and what wasn't. When I grew tired, she sighed and said that she had not had much schooling in Germany, found it hard to speak and understand English, but was doing better in Italian. I said I would give her English lessons if she would teach me German or Italian and Bethe said she would inquire if that would be allowed.

I have no memory of when we saw each other again because the next meeting is merged with the others that followed, that year and the three or four years before she disappeared once more. I think in those years I saw her eight or nine times, but nothing now is clear to me except a few sharp pictures and sounds: I know that I told her about the Druids and that I gave her my copy of *Bleak House* and that she returned it, shaking her head; she brought me a photograph of her father and mother, and I know that only because I still have it; once we went to the movies and a man behind us touched her shoulder and she pressed his hand; I brought along my English grammar and tried, one day in Audubon Park, to explain the pluperfect as she stared at me, solemn, struggling, and I touched the beautiful, heavy auburn hair to console her and to apologize. I know that led to sad, sympathetic talk about my hair, blonde and shameless straight in a time when it was fashionable to have curls. And one Sunday, when I went to the corner store, she rolled my hair in wet toilet paper rolls and put a scarf around my head, saying that would do it, and after we had gone to sit in a Catholic church where the priest near the poor box seemed to know her, and we had not spoken for a long time, she unwrapped my curlers, and as the hair came from the curlers as loose and dank as always, she kissed me. It was not a good thing to do. I disliked Bethe for thinking I was "unattractive," a word of my generation that meant you wouldn't ever marry. My friend Julia, in our New York school group of four strangely assorted girls, was too rich to think about marriage and I envied her. I was impractical: I wanted to marry a poet. One of us did marry a young poet but he killed himself a few months after the marriage over the body of his male lover.

On another Sunday morning I went to the store to tell Bethe that we would be leaving for New York in a few days. The young boy who always answered the bell said Bethe was in church and so I went looking for her. She was sitting with a tall, bald-headed man so dark of skin I thought he was a Negro. Something kept me from them and I turned to leave. But Bethe saw me. She said something to the man, he answered,

25

rose, and quickly moved ahead of her. She took my hand and we stood outside in the sun, waiting, I think, for the man to disappear.

She was trying to say something. Whenever she was ready to talk, she moved her lips as if rehearsing the words, and now I saw that what she was going to say she didn't want to say.

"Do not again come to church here, *Liebchen*."

"I'm sorry."

"You are not Catholic. Some do not like it so, your coming."

"But you are not Catholic, either."

"I am. I become. I believe now God, Father, Holy Ghost."

I was accustomed to my mother's religiosity, a woman seeking and believing that salvation lay in the God of any church. My mother, therefore, had no church, calling in at many; but now, with Bethe, I recognized the assertive tone of the uncommitted because I had so long heard the tone of the committed.

In those days I said whatever came into my head, in any manner that my head formed the idea and the words. (It is, indeed, strange to write of your own past. "In those days" I have written, and will leave here, but I am not at all sure that those days have been changed by time. All my life I believed in the changes I could, and sometimes did, make in a nature I so often didn't like, but now it seems to me that time made alterations and mutations rather than true reforms; and so I am left with so much of the past that I have no right to think it very different from the present.)

I said to Bethe before I began to cry, "You lie because a man tells you to."

She stared at me, walked ahead of me, motioned to me to follow. We went back to the corner store and she disappeared into the back room and reappeared immediately to ask me if I would like to have a good Italian lunch in a good Italian restaurant.

I could now, I did a few years ago, walk to that restaurant; I could make a map of the tables and the faces that were there that Sunday, so long ago. Freud said that people could not remember smells, they could only be reminded of them, but I still believe I remember the odor of boiling salt water, the close smell of old wine stains. I had never been in such a place. Somewhere I knew I was on the edge of acquisition, a state of nervousness which often caused me to move my hands and wrists as if I were entering into a fit.

Bethe asked me what I wanted to eat, I shook my head, she ordered in Italian from a thin old lady who seemed to know her. We had a heavy sauce poured over something I could not identify and did not like. (The food in our house was good: at one end of the serving table there was always the New Orleans cooking of my father's childhood and, at the other, the Negro backwoods stuff of my mother's Alabama black-earth land. Food in other places seemed inferior.) This Italian food was a mess.

I don't know how long it took me to search each face in the restaurant with the eagerness the young have for strangers in strange places, nor how long it took me to recognize the man who had been in church with Bethe. He was sitting alone at a table, staring at a wall, as if to keep his face from us. I asked Bethe for a glass of water and found her staring at the man, her lips compressed as if to hold the mouth from doing something else, her shoulders rigid against the chair. The man turned from the wall, the eyes dropped to the table, and then the head went up suddenly and stared at Bethe until the lips took on the look of her lips and the shoulders went back against the chair with the same sharp intake of muscles. Before any gesture was made, I knew I was seeing what I had never seen before and, since like most only children, all that I saw related to me, I felt a sharp pain as if I were alone in the world and always would be. As she raised her hand to her mouth and then turned the palm toward him, I pushed the heavy paste stuff in front of me so far across the table that it turned and was on the tablecloth. She did not see what I had done because she was waiting for him as he rose from his chair. She went to meet him. When they reached each other, his hand went down her arm and she closed her eyes. As I ran out of the restaurant, I saw her go back to our table.

Hannah wrote to us in New York a few weeks later saying that Bethe had telephoned twice to ask for me, and wasn't that odd? My father wanted to know why

I thought Bethe had asked for *me*, but I had learned to smile at such questions and my father had learned that what had been childish bucking was, if pushed, turning into sharp, unpleasant stubbornness. We had had an uncomfortable winter; I was getting bad marks in school when, all my life, I had been given good ones; I was locking the door of my room and sometimes refusing to come out for meals; I was disappearing at odd hours, and questions about that were not answered. I had run away from home for a day and a night and was, as spring came, refusing to go back to the girls' camp where I had spent so many summers. And late one night I had tried to climb up ten fire escapes into my room to avoid my parents' questions on why I had cuts on my face. I didn't climb more than three fire escapes before the apartment house was in an uproar.

I did send Bethe a Christmas card, but I didn't see her on our next winter visit to New Orleans. It was to be the last regular visit we ever made. It was finally obvious to my parents that I couldn't be dragged back and forth from a bad school in New Orleans to a good school in New York: I was getting too old for such adjustments. I had, on that last visit, gone immediately to the corner store, but I did not ring the bell, telling myself I would come the next day. But I did not go back again.

I have very little memory of that winter in New Orleans or the summer in Biloxi, Mississippi. I know that I watched every movement that Carl Bowman, Junior, made as he dove off the pier, or pitched in the baseball game, or walked down our block, and one night I was wracked with gagging, the emotion was so great, as he put his arm around me. I must have thought about Bethe, because in my "writer's book" for that period I practiced a code based on her name, but now, looking at the book, I can't understand the code.

The last week of our visit — we had returned to New Orleans from Biloxi — we were sitting around Jenny's dining room table, her boarders having gone their after-dinner way, in the family hour that I always liked. My father was reading the paper, and when he made a sound in his throat I saw Jenny nudge Hannah. Hannah nodded, Jenny put down her sewing, Hannah closed her book, and they watched my father.

He said, "Well the boys are shooting it up again. Have you seen her?"

Jenny said, "No."

"Who?" asked my mother.

"Stay away from her," my father said to Jenny, "do you hear me?"

"Stay away from whom?" said my mother. "What are you talking about?"

My father turned his chair toward Hannah. "Stay away from her, I tell you. These boys are nothing to fool around with."

My mother's voice, soft, rose now to high. "It's always been like this."

Hannah, who liked my mother, whispered, "Now, Julia, he will tell you — "

But I was trying hard to listen to my father and Jenny, knowing from long experience that they would have the interesting things to say, the opinions by which the other two would abide. Jenny had said something I missed, was saying now, "Not for two years, maybe more, although one day I saw her in a car, a *car*, an automobile, I mean, and I hurried over — "

"Don't do that again," said my father. "Don't hurry over. If she comes here, say you're sorry, or whatever you can say that will curb your curiosity."

"Mind your business," Jenny laughed.

"I don't care who she sleeps with," said my father, "nor how many. I care that this one is a danger and you're not to go near her with any excuses to me later on."

"It is my belief," said Jenny, "that Hannah and I earn our own living — "

"Oh, shut up that stuff," said my father, "and be serious. These boys are killers."

"Killers," said my mother. "It's always been like this. You never answer me, I'm never told the secrets."

"O.K.," said my father, "you have relatives who are killers."

"Whatever you think of them," said my mother, "my family are *not* killers and even you have never said that in all the years."

"Oh, Julia," said Hannah, "you always let him tease you. You always do."

"What a sucker," said Jenny.

"Don't interfere between man and wife," my father said. "What is it you want to know, Julia?"

"My relatives are not killers and you ought not to say so in front of our child."

My father turned to me. "Your mother's family are not killers of white people. Remember that and be proud. They never do more than beat up niggers who can't pay fifty percent interest on the cotton crop and that's how they got rich."

"The child has no respect now," said my mother, "for my family."

"I didn't say *your* family were killers. I said you were now *related* to killers."

"Oh, God," said Jenny to my mother, "he means us, *our* cousin, Bethe."

"In a proper marriage," said my father, "the blood of one house merges with the blood of the other, or have I misunderstood the marriage vows?"

"You've misunderstood them when you wanted to," said Jenny, and Hannah rose nervously and puttered about. Then my father said something to Jenny in German and I couldn't understand much of it, although I could have managed more if my mother hadn't kept on saying, "Please translate for me," and "That isn't nice. You know I can't understand," and, "Very well, ignore me," until my father said to her, "Bethe's common-law husband, if that's the word," and Jenny said, *"Schweigen vor dem Kind,"* and everybody was silent.

I said, "I will go to bed now so you won't have to

Schweigen vor dem Kind and I've known what that's
meant since I was three years old."

"You're smart," Jenny said, "but if you were
smarter you wouldn't have told us that."

An hour later, when all the lights were out, I came
down to the dining room and found the newspaper.
There was a long story about the beating up of some
men with Italian names because they were running
bootleg liquor, and the headline included the name
Arneggio and said he and his brother were being
sought by the police in a suspected gang warfare.

At breakfast the next morning I said to my father,
"Arneggio is the man in the corner store. You ought
to help Bethe."

My father waited a long time, twice put up his hand
to silence Jenny. "What corner store? What are you
talking about?"

I had made a mistake and I was angry with myself.
"I don't know. But you ought to help Bethe. She loves
him."

"Come out on the porch," said my father.

"I'm late for church."

"*Church?* What church?"

"To understand is to forgive," I said, "and love she
does, and so does he, and to her aid you must go."

"My God," said Jenny, "help us."

"It's *you* who have taught our child to go to any
church and talk that way," my father said to my
mother as he took me by the arm. "Come outside and
let's have a talk."

"You will bully me," I yelled to my father, who never had, "or you will trick me. And both are immoral and I will not say one more word to a Philistine."

I was at my high-class moral theory stage, from which I have never completely emerged, and I had even had time to learn that it often worked.

"Immoral," I shouted as I ran from the room.

"That's not nice, baby," said my mother, looking in another direction.

"Immoral," I shouted, and sulked under the fig tree, refusing lunch, until late in the day when I asked permission to visit Grace Alberts, the daughter of my father's best friend, crippled at birth from the syphilis of her father. When Jenny said that was very strange because I had often said I didn't like cripples, my mother told Jenny that perhaps I was growing more charitable and she thought the visit to poor Grace was a good idea.

I knew where I was going — the house dictionary having failed me — so I stopped by Christy Houghton's on my way. Christy was the daughter of divorced parents, necked openly with the boys, and was two years older than I. I wanted to ask her what a common-law wife was. She explained it was a fancy name for just a plain old whore in this wide, wide world. The third time she said whore I twisted her arm and held it firm as I forced her to repeat after me, "Does love need a minister, a rabbi, a priest? Is divine love between man and woman based on permission of a decadent society?" and would not now believe those words except I liked them so much that they are written three times in my "writer's book."

When I left Christy Houghton she screamed after me that everybody knew about Bethe Bowman from the newspapers and I came from a family of gangster-whores. (One of the few clear memories I have of the opening night of *The Children's Hour*, almost fifteen years later, is Christy Houghton kissing me and saying, "I married a New Yorker. You're drunk, aren't you?")

But that day I went down to the corner store. It was boarded up and nobody answered the bell. I paced around the block and tried again, worried that I had lost Bethe forever. I took a page from my notebook, wrote a message, and slipped it under the door. As I walked back to the streetcar, a man behind me called, "Hey, young lady," and I began to run. He caught me easily after a block and made sure by a very firm hold on my arm that I couldn't move.

"What's your name?"

I was too frightened to answer. After a minute he took my small purse and went through it to find almost nothing except cigarette butts and my "writer's book."

"What are you doing at Arneggio's place?"

"Nothing."

"Nothing? You don't know the people?"

"I'm on my way home."

"I'll come along with you."

I said, "Please," didn't like myself for it, and heard the fear turn into anger. "Please take your hand off my arm. I don't like to be held down."

He laughed and with that laugh caused a lifelong, often out-of-control hatred of cops, in all circumstances, in all countries. Then the grip lessened and he said, "Nobody's out to hurt you. What's this mean?"

He held out the paper I had put under the door. I had written, "Stendhal said love made people brave, dear Bethe."

"Stendhal was a writer," I started, "who — "

"What do you know about the dame?"

"The *dame?* The *dame?*"

"Look, kid, what were you doing there?"

"Nothing. I told you. I just rang the bell — "

"What's your name and where do you live? Hurry up."

"I am on my way to church — "

I moved away from him. He let me go, or so I thought, until I got off the streetcar on St. Charles Avenue and saw him behind me. He smiled and waved at me and I turned around and got on the Jackson crosstown car. I had a soda in Kramer's Drug Store, felt better for it, and walked home.

Jenny and Hannah were waiting for me on the porch. Jenny motioned me back to the chicken coops, away from the house. She said, "The police were here. Fortunately, we all went to school with Emile. Why don't you mind your God-damned business?"

"No sense getting angry," Hannah said, "no sense."

"Why not? Why not get angry? Miss Busybody here — "

"Tell us," said Hannah.

"Does Papa know the police were here?"

"No. Not yet. But he gets to Memphis tonight."

"Then telephone him," I said, "and don't threaten me. I wasn't doing anything. I was looking for Bethe."

"Bethe? What for?"

Somewhere I knew why, but I didn't want to talk about it, and when they knew I wasn't going to answer, Jenny sailed back to the house and Hannah followed her. When I came in the door the phone was ringing, and as Jenny answered it she put up her hand to stop me from climbing the stairs. When she finished listening she said, "Very well," hung up, went across the room, and whispered to Hannah. I had never seen her face twitch before and was not to see it happen again until a day, many years later, when she first saw my father after he had been confined for senile dementia. It is not good to see people who have been pretending strength all their lives lose it even for a minute.

Hannah said, softly, "Well, don't let's make a fuss. Let's just go."

Jenny said to me, "Go wash your face. Put on a hat. Tell your mother we're taking a cake to Old Lady Simmons. And hurry."

When I came downstairs a taxi was waiting in front of the door. I had never seen my aunts take a taxi before. I think I knew where we were going, because when we drove up in front of police headquarters I wasn't surprised, although I must have taken such a sharp breath that Hannah took my hand.

Jenny, as always, went through the door first, and up to a man at the desk. "I'm Jenny Hellman. Tell Mr. Emile we're here."

"He's pretty busy," said the man, "pretty busy. Is that the girl?"

"Don't speak in that tone," said Jenny. "What is it you want with this child?"

"Is she a child?" said the man, and I thought of the Infant Phenomenon and laughed out of nervousness.

"Sit down, ladies," and the man rang a bell. Hannah gave me her handkerchief as we sat waiting on the bench and I said to her, "I love you."

"Oh, certainly, love is just what we need," said Jenny. "Give Hannah back that handkerchief. It was our mother's."

A man came out of an office, motioned us toward the door.

This time it was Hannah who said, "We'd like to see Mr. Emile. We went to school with him and he's been to our house all his life."

"He told me," said the man. "He isn't here. He's very busy." He turned to me. "How well did you know Al Arneggio?"

I was so surprised that I didn't answer until he repeated the question.

"I didn't know him. I never saw him — I saw him in a restaurant once."

"Who do you think we are," Jenny said, "knowing people like that?"

"I think you're nice ladies whose cousin lives with a man like that, that's what I think," said the man.

"*Schweigen vor dem Kind*," Hannah said. "I mean that isn't a nice way to talk in front of a young, very young girl."

The man said to me, "What were you doing at that place? At the store? Don't you know it isn't a store?"

"It's a kind of funny store. But it's got some things in it and — "

"How many times have you been there?"

I was growing very frightened, perhaps more of the look on Jenny's face than of the man or the place.

"I don't know how many. I only went to see Bethe."

"Why did you go today? Did you have a message?"

"A message? No, sir. Bethe never wanted my parents or my aunts to know."

"To know what?"

"Where she lived, I guess."

"Or the gangster she lived with?" he said to my aunts.

"We've known," said Hannah. "A man in my office told me. I hope her poor papa is dead long since. In Mannheim, Germany, I mean, he must be."

The man said, "I want to know why the girl went there today."

"I do, too," said Jenny, "although she meant no harm, she never does mean any harm, she is just too nosy and moves about — "

He stood in front of me now. "Why did you go there today?"

I had already come near a truth I couldn't name, so close to it, so convinced that something was being pushed up from the bottom of me, that I began to tremble with an anxiety I had never felt before. It had nothing to do with my fear of the policeman or of my family.

"Answer me, young lady. Why did you go there today?"

My voice was high and came, I thought, from somebody else.

"I don't know. I read about Mr. Arneggio last night. Love, I think, but I'm not sure."

A long time later somebody, I don't remember who, repeated the word love, and I heard Jenny's voice and the man's voice, but I was so busy gripping my knees that I couldn't, didn't, want to look up, or to hear, and didn't care what they said. Somewhere, during that time, I found out that pieces of Arneggio had been discovered a few hours before in the backyard of the store, and I heard the man say to my aunts, "O.K. I'll tell Mr. Emile. But if you should hear anything about Bethe Bowman it is your duty, the Mafia and all, dangerous, and keep the kid away from there."

Hannah it was who poked me to my feet and said to the man, "Thank you. You are most courteous."

I don't think we spoke on the streetcar going home but I don't know because I think of it now as the closest I have ever come to a conscious semiconsciousness, as if I were coming through an anesthetic, not back into a world of reality, but into a new body and time, moving toward something, running back at the moment I could have reached it. I am sure my aunts believed that I was frightened of police consequences or my father's anger. I was glad they thought that and nothing more. Later that night Jenny said that since Emile had not phoned she saw no sense in ever telling my father or mother if I would promise to stay away from Bethe.

The next day and for days after that there were discussions of the murder of Arneggio. Bethe's name was mentioned in every press story but she was never called Bowman. In the boardinghouse so many questions were asked, opinions exchanged, that Jenny grew very sharp and took to defending Bethe, perhaps out of family pride, perhaps from the tangles of her own nature, so sure, so dismissive of "the ninnies of this world," and so sympathetic to them.

From the time I was fourteen until I was twenty-five, I had no news of Bethe, although I often thought of her. I thought of her as I got dressed for my wedding, deliberately putting aside the pretty dress that was intended and choosing an old ugly gray chiffon. As it went over my head, I heard myself say her name, and I saw again the man, Arneggio, in the restaurant. Then I don't believe I ever thought of her again through a pleasant marriage that was not to last, until the first afternoon I slept with Dashiell Hammett.

As I moved toward the bed I said, "I'd like to tell you about my cousin, a woman called Bethe."

Hammett said, "You can tell me if you have to, but I can't say I would have chosen this time."

Later that same year I went to New York from Hollywood to tell my parents about my divorce, and then, on my way back to California, I went to New Orleans to tell my aunts. It was an unpleasant errand: my parents and my aunts liked my husband, knew that I liked him, and had every right to be puzzled and disturbed about me.

I suppose, in an effort not to talk about the present time, my aunts and I talked a good deal about past times, and it was on that visit, as I opened a closet door to get a bath towel, that I saw once again the canvas valise that had been given me and then taken back. As my aunts moved about the kitchen I stood staring at it, wondering about me and them. I wrapped a towel around me and went to stand in the kitchen door.

I said, "Is the letter still there from Bethe? The one that says she now has good Italian friend and that maybe if they marry you will come again to see her?"

Hannah turned her back to me. Jenny said, "What does all that old stuff mean now?"

"It means that long before the day at the police station you knew about Bethe and Arneggio. But you didn't tell me you knew."

"That's right," said Jenny. "Why don't you put on a bathrobe?"

But I wanted to have a fight, or to pay them back, because that night I said, "I know that you will not approve of my living with a man I am not married to, but that's the way it's going to be."

"How do you know that," said Jenny, "how do you know the difference between fear and approve?"

"Because you deserted, sorry, you gave Bethe up, when she loved a way you didn't like. When she was in trouble, neither of you, or Papa, went to help her."

An hour later, reading on my bed, I heard through the walls of the small shoddy house an argument between my aunts. There was nothing remarkable about that — Jenny's temper was as bad as my father's and mine — but something was different, and as I opened my door I realized that it was Hannah who was angry. Neither I nor anybody else, I think, had ever heard Hannah angry, and so I walked into the dining room to find out about it.

Jenny said to me, "Your generation, camp and college and all those fine places, goes about naked all the time?"

"Yes," I said, "all the time. And we sleep with everybody and drink and dope all night and don't have your fine feelings. Maybe that's the reason we don't always spit on people because they live with low-down Wops and get in trouble. Each generation has its standards."

Jenny laughed, but Hannah rose, turned over her chair and said, "Sit down."

Jenny said to her, "We don't have to prove ourselves."

"Why don't you go out in the garden?" Hannah asked Jenny, and as I whistled in surprise at the tone, she turned into her bedroom. I could see she was unlocking a box. Something large had happened between them. I went to get dressed and stalled to give them time.

When I came out, Jenny said to Hannah, "O.K. Go ahead."

Hannah handed me an open savings bank deposit book and said, "Look at the date on that page."

The date was ten years before, in the first days of September. There was a thousand-dollar withdrawal from a total of thirty-three hundred.

I said I didn't understand. Jenny said, "Hannah doesn't want you to think mean of her ever because she loves you more than sense. I, myself, don't give much of a damn what you think. But so be it. That thousand dollars was withdrawn about a week after the police station visit and was used to get Bethe out of trouble. Your father didn't know, nobody knew, and you're to shut up about it."

"You are fine ladies," I said after a while, "the best."

Jenny was angry. "Sure, sure, now put all that sweet-time patter in the shit can."

"My!" said Hannah.

Jenny said, "Bethe paid it back. A long time ago, after she sold the jewelry and other stuff he gave her and when the police finally left her alone, so don't start any stuff about you giving us the money because we are poor virgin ladies."

"I haven't got any money," I said, "but maybe someday."

"Then someday send us a steak."

"I will," I said. (The morning after *The Children's Hour* opened, four years later, I gave a porter on the Southern Pacific ten dollars to carry a package of twelve steaks to my aunts and got back a telegram saying, "Do we have to eat the porter as well?")

The next morning Hannah, who usually left for work at seven-thirty, was still in the dining room at eight-thirty, and as I ate the wonderful breakfast that brought back my childhood — tripe, biscuits, cold crabs, crawfish, bitter coffee — she said that she was entitled to a day's holiday when I came to visit. An hour later, Jenny appeared and said, "Come along, it's a long trolley ride."

I think I guessed where we were going, but I know so little about directions, and the city was so changed and grown, that I didn't bother to ask what direction we traveled in. When we reached the end of the trolley line, we began a long, long walk through flat, ugly, treeless land. Occasionally we would pass a small house, and once an old man came from a dilapidated outhouse to look at us. My aunts were tall, heavy women who never walked more than a few blocks, and now I heard Jenny's heavy breathing and became nervous when I saw Hannah take her hand. Near the

end of the road, sitting alone on the plain, was a
mean cottage, square against the sun. The half-
finished porch had four tilted steps and a broken chair
as if to show that somebody had once intended to use
it but had grown weary of the effort. Bethe was standing on the steps, her body slanted with their angle,
and I stopped at the handsome sight of her. She
came down the steps to support Jenny with one arm,
Hannah with the other. I followed them into the
house.

I don't think many words were spoken that afternoon, and certainly I said none of them. We drank a
bitter, black iced tea, we stayed about an hour, we
made the long trek home with sighs from Jenny as
Hannah hummed something or other off key. That
night I telephoned Dash to say I would stay in New
Orleans a few days longer, would return to Los Angeles on the weekend.

The next morning I went back to Bethe's, losing my
way on the turn of the dirt road, then finding it again.
As I came toward her house, I turned and ran from it,
around another dirt path and then off into another,
coming suddenly into a green place, swampy, with
heavy stump trees and large elephant ears. I heard
things jump in the swamp and I remember thinking
I must be sick without feeling sick, feverish without
fever. I don't know how long I ran, but a path brought
me in sight of a roof and as I ran toward it, thinking
that I must leave the sun and ask for water, I saw
Bethe hanging clothes from a line that stretched from

a pole to an outhouse. She was naked and I stopped to admire the proportions of the figure: the large hips, the great breasts, the tumbled auburn hair that came from the beautiful side of my father's family and, so I thought that day, had been lost in America. She must have heard the sound of the wet, ugly soil beneath me, because she turned, put her hands over her breasts, then moved them down to cover her vagina, then took them away to move the hair from her face.

I said, "It was you who did it. I would not have found it without you. Now what good is it, tell me that?"

She took a towel from the line, came toward me, and wiped my face. Then she took my hand, we went into the house, she pushed me gently into a chair. After a while she came back into the room, covered now by a cheap sack of a dress, carrying coffee. I must have fallen asleep in the chair because I came awake saying something, losing it, then trying to remember what I had wanted to say. I took a sip of the coffee, finished the cup and, for the first time in my grown life, I vomited. Then I must have gone back to sleep because when I looked down the floor was clean and Bethe was in the kitchen. I went to stand near her as she dropped heavy-looking dough balls into a boiling broth.

She asked me, half in German, half in English, how I was feeling. I tried to say I had never felt sick and, trying too hard, said, "I wasn't sick. Just the opposite. It was that day in the restaurant, you and Arneggio — " and never finished, because as I spoke the man's name she put her hand over my mouth. When she took it away she said, "Now I go in bed maybe seven or eight P.M., in the night. He is plumber and like dinner when come home soon at four-thirty in afternoon. Come for visit again."

I waited for a dumpling to be finished, ate it, didn't like it, shook hands with Bethe, and walked down the road. Not far from the larger dirt road that would join the road of the streetcar back to New Orleans, I passed a very thin middle-aged man, carrying a lunch pail. Maybe he wasn't the plumber, but I think he was.

I was never to find out. Two years later my aunts wrote that Bethe died of pneumonia and they had only known about it because they had a note from a T. R. Carter. They said things like poor Bethe and they wished they had been able to help her, but they were getting old and the streetcar ride was hard for them, although they had always sent a present at Christmas and what they thought was her birthday. My aunts said they had written to Germany, had no reply, didn't know if any of Bethe's family were still alive, but maybe the next time I went to Germany I would try to find out and bring the news.

I never went back to Germany because now it was the time of Hitler, and I don't even remember talking again about Bethe with my aunts, although one drunken night I did try to tell Hammett about Bethe, and got angry when he said he didn't understand what

I meant when I kept repeating that Bethe had had a lot to do with him and me. I got so angry that I left the apartment, drove to Montauk on a snowy day, and came back two days later with the grippe.

WILLY

H E was married to my ridiculous great-aunt. But I was sixteen or seventeen by the time I knew she was ridiculous, having before then thought her most elegant. Her jewelry, the dresses from Mr. Worth in Paris, her hand-sewn underwear with the Alençon lace, her Dubonnet with a few drops of spirits of ammonia, were all fine stuff to me. But most of all, I was impressed with her silences and the fineness of her bones.

My first memory of Aunt Lily — I was named for her; born Pansy, she had changed it early because, she told me, "Pansy was a tacky old darky name" — is of watching one of the many fine lavallières swing between the small bumps of her breasts. How, I asked myself in those early years of worship, did my mother's family ever turn out anything so "French," so *raffinée?* It was true that her family were all thin people, and all good-looking, but Lily was a wispy, romantic specimen unlike her brothers and sisters, who were high-spirited and laughed too much over their own vigor and fancy money deals.

That is what I thought about Aunt Lily until I made the turn and the turn was as sharp as only the young can make when they realize their values have been shoddy. It was only then that I understood about the Dubonnet and recognized that the lavallières were too elaborate for the ugly dryness of the breasts, and thought the silences coma-like and stupid. But that, at least, was not the truth.

Lily was so much younger than her brothers and sisters, one of whom was my grandmother, that I don't think she was more than ten years older than my mother. It was whispered that her mother had given birth to her at sixty, and in my bewitched period that made her Biblical and in my turn-against period made her malformed.

I do not know her age or mine when I first met her, because she and her husband, Willy, their son and daughter, had been living in Mobile, and had only then, at the time of my meeting them, moved back to New Orleans. I think I was about nine or ten and I know they lived in a large house on St. Charles Avenue filled with things I thought beautiful and foreign, only to realize, in my turn-against period, that they were ornate copies of French and Italian miseries, cluttering all the tables and running along the staircase walls and newel posts on up to the attic quarters of Caroline Ducky.

Whenever we visited Aunt Lily I was sent off to Caroline Ducky with a gift of chocolate-covered cherries or a jar of pickles, because Caroline Ducky was part of my mother's childhood. Anyway, I liked her. She was an old, very black lady who had been born into slavery in my mother's family and, to my angry eyes, didn't seem to want to leave it. She occupied only part of the large attic and did what was called "the fine sewing," which meant that she embroidered initials on handkerchiefs and towels and Uncle Willy's shirts and was the only servant in the house allowed to put an iron to Aunt Lily's clothes. Caroline Ducky never came downstairs: her meals were brought to her by her daughter, Flo Ducky. Whatever I learned about that house, in the end, came mostly from Caroline Ducky, who trusted me, I think, because my nurse Sophronia was her niece and Sophronia had vouched for me at an early age. But then her own daughter, Flo Ducky, was retarded and was only allowed to deal with the heavy kitchen pans. There were many other servants in that house, ten, perhaps, but I remember only Caroline Ducky and a wheat-colored chauffeur called Peters. Peters was a fine figure in gray uniform, very unlike my grandmother's chauffeur, who was a mean-spirited slob of a German mechanic without any uniform. My grandmother and the other sister, Hattie, would often discuss Peters in a way that was clear to me only many years later, but even my innocent mother would often stop talking when Peters came into the room with Aunt Lily's Dubonnet or to suggest a cooling drive to Lake Pontchartrain.

Aunt Lily's daughter died so early after they returned to New Orleans that I do not even remember what she looked like. It was said officially that she died of consumption, supposedly caused by her insistence on sleeping on the lawn, but when anybody in my mother's family died there was always the rumor of syphilis. In any case, after her daughter's death, Aunt Lily never again appeared in a "color" — all her clothes, for the rest of her life, were white, black, gray and purple and, I believed in the early days, another testament to her world of sensibility and the heart.

The son was called Honey and to this day I do not know any other name for him. (He died about fifteen years ago in a loony bin in Mobile and there's nobody left to ask his real name.) Honey looked like his mother, thin-boned, yellowish, and always sat at dinner between Lily and his father, Uncle Willy, to "interpret" for them.

I suppose I first remember Willy at the dinner table, perhaps a year after they had moved to New Orleans, although because he was a legend I had heard about him all my life. For years I thought he was a legend only to my family, but as I grew up I realized that he was a famous character to the rest of the city, to the state, and in certain foreign parts. Depending, of course, on their own lives and natures, people admired him, envied him, or were frightened of him: in my mother's family his position in a giant corporation, his demotions, his reinstatements, his borrowings, his gamblings, were, as Jake, my grandmother's brother, said, "a sign of a nation more interested in charm than in stability, the road to the end." By which my grandmother's brother meant that Willy had gone beyond their middle-class gains made by cheating Negroes on cotton crops. But, in fairness to her family, I was later to discover that Willy had from time to time borrowed a large part of Lily's fortune, made money with it, lost it, returned it, borrowed it again, paid interest on it, and finally, by the time I met him, been refused it altogether.

I do not think that is the only reason Aunt Lily and her husband no longer spoke to one another, but that's what Honey's "interpretations" seemed to be about. Uncle Willy, his pug, good-looking, jolly face, drawn by nature to contrast with my aunt's sour delicacy, would say to Honey such things as, "Ask your mother if I may borrow the car, deprive her of Peters for a few hours, to go to the station. I will be away for two weeks, at the Boston office." Honey would repeat the message word for word to his mother on the other side of him and, always after a long silence, Aunt Lily would shrug and say, "Tell your father he does not need to ask for his car. *His* money bought it. I would have been happier with something more modest."

There were many "interpretations" about trips or

cars, but the day of that particular one, Willy looked down at his plate for a long time and then, looking up, laughed at my mother's face. "Julia, Julia," he said. "You are the charming flower under the feet of the family bulls." Then, puzzling to a child, his laughter changed to anger and he rose, threw his napkin in Honey's face and said, "Tell your mother to buy herself another more modest car. Tell her to buy it with a little piece of the high interest she charged me for the loan she made." We stayed for a longer time than usual that day, although Lily didn't speak again, but on the way home my mother stopped in the nearest church, an old habit when she was disturbed, any church of any belief, and I waited outside, impatient, more than that, the way I always was.

Aunt Jenny, my father's sister, who ran a boarding-house, would take me each Saturday to the French market for the weekly food supplies. It was our custom to have lunch in the Quarter at Tujague's, and my watered wine and her unwatered wine always made for a nice time. And so the next day after Willy had told my mother she was a charming flower, I said to Jenny, "Everybody likes Mama, don't they?"

"Almost," she said, "but not you. You're jealous of your mama and you ought to get over that before it's too late."

"Mama nags," I said. "Papa understands."

"*Ach.* You and your papa. Yes, she does nag. But she doesn't know it and is a nice lady. I said you must know your mother before it is too late."

She was right. By the time I knew how much I loved my mother and understood that her eccentricities were nothing more than that and could no more be controlled than the blinking of an eye in a high wind, it was, indeed, too late. But I didn't like lectures even from Jenny.

"Uncle Willy likes Mama," I said. "I think that's hard for Aunt Lily."

Jenny stared at me. "Hard for *Lily?* Hard for your Aunt Lily?"

"You don't like her because she's thin," I said to Jenny, who was six feet tall, and heavy, and had long been telling me that my rib bones showed. "I think she's the most interesting, the only interesting, part of our family."

"Thank you," said Jenny. "Your *mother's* family. Not mine."

"I didn't mean you or Hannah," I said, "really, I . . ."

"Don't worry," Jenny said as she rose, "about me, worry about yourself and why you like very thin people who have money."

I asked her what she meant, and she said that someday she would tell me if I didn't find out for myself. (I did find out, and when I told her she laughed and said I was thirty years old, but better late than never.)

It was that year, the year of my mother being a flower, and now, in my memory, the year before my sharp turn, that I saw most of Aunt Lily. I went to

the house two or three times a week and whatever she
was doing, and she was never doing much, she would
put aside to give me hot chocolate, sending Honey to
another room as if she and I were ready to exchange
the pains of women. I usually went in the late after-
noons, after school, but sometimes I was invited to
Saturday lunch. The visits were hung in a limbo of
fog over water, but I put that down to the way people
who had greater culture and sensibility than the rest
of us lived their special lives. I don't know what I
meant by culture: in Aunt Lily's house there were no
books other than a set of Prescott, and once when
Jenny and I went to our second-balcony seats for a
concert of Verdi's *Requiem* Aunt Lily sent for us to
join her in her box. After a while, Jenny said to me,
"Would you ask your Cultivated Majesty Aunt please
not to hum the Wedding March? It doesn't go well
with the 'Libera me' and there are other reasons she
should forget it." But I put that down to Jenny's cus-
tomary sharpness and went on with my interest in
Aunt Lily.

Ever since her daughter's death Aunt Lily made
soft sounds from time to time and talked even less
than before, although unconnected phrases like "lost
life," "the hopes of youth," "inevitable waste," would
come at intervals. I was never sure whether she was
talking of her daughter or of herself, but I did know
that, for a woman who had never before used her
hands, she now often touched my hair, patted my arm,
or held Honey firmly by the hand.

And I thought it was the need to deny the death of her child that made possible the scene I once saw when I arrived for a visit while Lily was out shopping. The car came into the driveway to the side door and from the window I saw Peters reach in for Lily's hand. As she stepped from the car, she twisted and slipped. Peters caught her and carried her to the door. On the way there, her head moved down to kiss his hair.

I did not know how to cross the room away from the window, how to face what I had seen, so I ran up to the third floor to call upon Caroline Ducky. Past the second landing I heard Honey's voice behind me. He said, "He does it to her."

"Does what?"

"You're older than me," he said, and ran up ahead of me. He was larger, taller than I, and his face was now sweaty and vacant.

I said, "What's the matter?"

"Ssh and I'll show it to you."

I went by him and was caught by the arm. "Want to see it?"

"See what?"

"My thingy."

I hadn't seen a thingy since I was four years old and maybe my no came too slow, because my shoulders were held with his one hand, my dress lifted with the other, and I felt something knocking against my stomach.

"Open up," he shouted into his future. "Open up."

I sneezed so hard that he fell back against the staircase wall. I was subject to sneezing fits and now I stood in the full force of one violent rack after another. When the sneezing was over, Honey had disappeared and Caroline Ducky was standing a few steps above me. I don't know how long she had been there but I followed her to the attic, was told to press my upper lip and given a Coca-Cola spiced heavily with spirits of ammonia, an old and perhaps dangerous New Orleans remedy for anything you didn't understand.

Caroline Ducky looked up from her sewing. "You be careful of that Honey." (She was to be right: at twenty he raped a girl at a picnic, at twenty-two or -three he was sued by a Latvian girl for assault, and his later years in the Mobile loony bin were in some way connected with an attack on a woman who was fishing in the Dog River.)

Caroline Ducky said, "I knew what he was going to be the day it took him three days to get himself out."

"Out of what?"

"Out of the stomach of his mother."

"What did you know?"

"I knew what I knew."

I laughed with an old irritation. Such answers were, perhaps still are, a Southern Negro form of put-down to the questions of white people.

"His mama didn't want him, his papa didn't want him, and a child nobody wants got nothing ahead but seeping sand."

"Then what did they have him for? They don't like each other."

"She trapped him," said Caroline Ducky. "Mr. Willy, he was drunk."

"Things can't start from birth, that early," I said from the liberalism I was learning.

"That ain't early, the day you push out, that's late."

"What did you mean Aunt Lily trapped him? How can a man be trapped?"

"You too young for the question, I too old for the answer." She was pleased with herself and laughed.

"Then what did you start it for? You all do that. It's rotten mean."

Grown people were always on the edge of telling you something valuable and then withdrawing it, a form of bully-teasing. (Little of what they withdrew had any value, but the pain of learning that can be unpleasant.) And I was a particular victim of this empty mystery game because, early and late, an attempt was made to hide from me the contempt of my mother's family for my father's lack of success, and thus there was a kind of patronizing pity for me and my future. I think I sensed that mystery when I was very young and to protect what little I had to protect I constructed the damaging combination that was not to leave me until I myself made money: I rebelled against my mother's family, and thus all people who were rich, but I was frightened and impressed by them; and the more frightened and impressed I grew the more aimless became my anger, which sometimes expressed itself in talk about the rights of Negroes and on two Sundays took the form of deliberately breaking plates at my grandmother's table. By fourteen my heart was with the poor except on the days when it was with those who ground them under. I remember that period as a hell of self-dislike, but I do not now mean to make fun of it: not too many years later, although old shriveled leaves remain on the stump to this day, I understood that I lived under an economic system of increasing impurity and injustice for which I, and all those like me, pay with ridiculous wounds to the spirit.

"What's rotten mean," asked Caroline Ducky, "you snip-talking girl?"

"Rotten mean, all of you."

"I like your Uncle Willy," she said, "but he ain't no man of God."

She closed her eyes and crossed herself and that meant my visit was finished. She was the only Baptist I ever knew who crossed herself and I doubt if she knew that she used the Greek cross. I left the house and went far out of my way to back-of-town, the Negro section, to put a dime in the poor box of the Baptist Church. I did this whenever I had an extra dime and years before, when my nurse Sophronia had proudly told my father about it, he said to me, "Why don't you give it to the Synagogue? Maybe we never told you that's where you belong." I said I couldn't do that because there was no synagogue for Negroes and my father said that was perfectly true, he'd never thought about that before.

For years I told myself that it was from that day, the day Caroline Ducky said he was no man of God, that I knew about Uncle Willy, but now I am not sure — diaries carry dates and pieces of conversation, but no record of family gossip — when I knew that he had been a poor boy in Mobile, Alabama, working young on the docks, then as a freight boss for a giant company doing business in Central America, and had married Lily when he was twenty-four and she was thirty. It was said that he had married her for money and respectability, but after six or seven years he couldn't have needed either because by that time he was vice-president of the company, living with the first fast cars, a hundred-foot yacht, the St. Charles Avenue great house, an apartment at the old Waldorf in New York, a hunting place on Jekyll Island, an open and generous hand with everybody, including, I think, my father in his bad years.

Sometimes in those years, years of transition for me, the dinner table of the St. Charles Avenue house included other guests — the "interpretations" of Honey between his mother and father still went on but were circumspect when these people were present — fine-looking, heavy men, with blood in their faces and sound to their voices, and then I heard talk of what they did and how they did it. I don't know when I understood it, or if anybody explained it to me, but there were high tales of adventure, with words like "good natives," "troublemakers," and the National City Bank, ships and shipments that had been sabotaged, teaching lessons to peons, and long, highly relished stories of a man called Christmas, a soldier of

65

fortune who worked for my uncle's company as a mercenary and had a great deal to do with keeping the peons quiet. At one dinner the talk was of "outbreaks," arranged by "native troublemakers" — two men who worked for my uncle's company had been murdered — and the need for firm action, revenge. The firm action was taken by Mr. Christmas, who strung up twenty-two men of a Guatemalan village, cut out their tongues, and burned down the village, driving the others into the jungle. Uncle Willy did not join in the pleasure of that tale, but he said nothing to stop it, nor to interfere with a plan to send a boatload of guns to Christmas to "insure the future."

The terrors and exploitations of this company were to become a world scandal, the first use of the U.S. Marines as private mercenaries to protect American capital. But even in my uncle's time, the scandal was of such proportions that the guns and the killings tapered off enough to convince me that the company had grown "liberal" as it established schools, decent houses and hospitals for the natives. When, in 1969, I told that to a graduate student from Costa Rica, he laughed and said he thought I should come and see for myself.

In any case, my reaction to those dinner tales at Aunt Lily's was an unpleasant mixture: my distaste for what I heard did not stop my laughter, when they laughed, at the shrewdness and heroics of "our boys" as they triumphed over the natives. I believed in Willy's personal affection and generosity toward the poor people he exploited. But the values of grown people had long pounded at my head, torn me apart with their contradictions.

But I could not now, in truth, get straight the tangled mess of that conflict which went so many years past my childhood: I know only that there were changes and that one day I felt that Aunt Lily was silly and that I had been a fool for ever thinking anything else. But I went on being sympathetic and admiring of Uncle Willy, interested in the days of his youth when he had ridden mules through Central and South American jungles, speaking always with an almost brotherly admiration of the natives from whom he "bought" the land. I am sure that his adventures made him interesting, the money he earned from them was different to me than money earned from a bank or a store, that his fall from high position seemed to me a protest, which it wasn't. And I had other feelings for him, although I didn't know about them for years after the time of which I speak.

But I already thought Aunt Lily foolish stuff the day of the outbreak. We had arrived in New Orleans only a few hours before she telephoned to ask my mother to come immediately. My mother said she was tired from the long journey, but that evidently didn't suit Aunt Lily because my mother told Jenny she guessed she'd have to go immediately, something bad must have happened. Jenny sniffed and said the something bad that had happened was probably the lateness of the Paris mails that failed to bring Aunt Lily's newest necklace. My mother said it was her duty to go and I said I would go along with her. Since I didn't often volunteer to go anywhere with my mother, she was pleased, and we set off at my mother's slow pace. Lily was pacing around her upstairs sitting room, her eyes blank and unfocused, and, annoyed with seeing me, she said immediately that it was too bad my hair was so straight and muddy-blonde, now that I was fourteen. But she sent for my hot chocolate and her watered Dubonnet, and my mother nervously chatted about our New York relatives until I went to a corner with a copy of *Snappy Stories*.

I guess Lily forgot about me because she said to my mother, "You've heard about Willy."

My mother said no, she hadn't heard about Willy, what was the matter, and Aunt Lily said, "I don't believe you. Jenny Hellman must have told you."

I don't think anybody in her life had ever before told my mother they didn't believe her, and I was amazed at the firmness with which she said that Jenny had told her nothing, Jenny didn't move in large circles, worked too hard, and she, my mother, always tried not to lie before God.

"God," said Aunt Lily. *"God?* He hasn't kept everybody else in town from lying at me. Me and Honey and my brothers and sisters who warned me early against Willy. It isn't the first time, but now it's in the open, now that he says he's paid me back when, of course, he still owes me sixty thousand," and she began to cry.

I saw my mother's face, the pity, the getting ready, and knew that she was going to walk into, be a part of, one of those messes the innocent so often walk into, make worse, and are victimized by. I left the room.

I met Peters in the hall. When he spoke to me, I realized he had never spoken to me before. "Miss Lily with your mama? Miss Lily upsetting herself?"

"I guess so," and started up the stairs toward Caroline Ducky.

"Miss Caroline Ducky don't feel good," he said. "I wouldn't bother her today." I went past him.

When Caroline Ducky answered my knock and we had kissed, I said, "Sorry you don't feel good. Your rheumatism?"

"One thing, five things. They mix around when you getting old. Sit you down and tell me what you reading."

This was an old habit between us. She liked stories and I would sum up for her a book I had read, making the plot more simple, cutting down the number of people, and always, as the story went on, she forgot it came from a book, thought it came from life, and would approve or disapprove. But I didn't want to fool around that day.

"What's Aunt Lily so upset about? She made Mama come right away. Something about Uncle Willy and the whole town knowing."

Caroline Ducky said, "The whole town don't know and don't care. Has to do with that Cajun girl, up Bayou Teche."

I was half crazy with pleasure, as I always was with this kind of stuff, but I had ruined it so many times before by going fast with questions that now I shut up. Caroline Ducky, after a while, handed me her embroidery hoop to work on and went to stand by her small window, leaning out to look at the street. In the last few years she had done this a good deal and I figured it had to do with age and never going into the street except for a funeral, and never liking a city where she had been made to live.

She said, over her shoulder, "I'm making a plan to die in high grass. All this Frenchy stuff in this town. Last night, I ask for greens and pot likker. That shit nigger at the stove send me up gumbo, Frenchy stuff. Tell your ma to cook me up some greens and bring 'em here. Your ma used to be a beauty on a wild horse. A wild Alabama horse."

I suppose there was something wrong with my face because she said, "Your ma's changed. City no good for country folk, your ma and me."

"What's that mean?"

"Your ma's a beauty inside out."

I didn't know why she was talking about my mother and I didn't want to talk about her that day, but I think Caroline Ducky meant that my mother was a country girl and the only comfortable period of her life had been with the Alabama Negroes of her childhood. New Orleans and New York, a worldly husband, a difficult child, unloving sisters and a mother of formidable coldness had made deep marks on my mother by the time I was old enough to understand her eccentric nature.

I said, "Uncle Willy going to marry a Cajun girl?"

"What? *What?* There ain't a white child born to woman ain't crazy," said Caroline Ducky. "Niggers sit around wasting time talk about white folk being pig-shit mean. Not me. All I ever say, they crazy. Lock up all white folk, give 'em to eat, but lock 'em up. Then all the trouble be over. What you talking about, *marry* Cajun girl?"

"All I meant was it must be kind of hard for Aunt Lily. Uncle Willy's being in love. I guess nobody wants to share their husband. My father isn't faithful to my mother."

"How you know that?"

"I found out years ago at a circus when . . ."

"Shut up," said Caroline Ducky, "this house pushing me to my grave."

There were sudden sounds from downstairs, as if somebody was calling. I opened Caroline Ducky's door but nobody seemed to be calling me, so I closed it again and went back to the embroidery hoop hoping to please Caroline Ducky into more talk, but the sounds downstairs grew louder and Caroline Ducky was too busy listening to pay any attention to anything I might ask.

She laughed. "Well, well. Time now for Miss Lily's morphine shot."

This was the richest hour I had ever spent and I was willing to try anything.

"Look, Caroline Ducky, I'll take you back to Demopolis. I'll get the money from Papa or I can sell my squirrel coat and books. I'll take you back, I swear."

"Shut the shit," said Caroline Ducky, good and mad. "Take me home! What I going to do when I get there? Nobody there for me except the rest of your shit catfish family. Home. What home I got?"

The door opened and Uncle Willy came in. "What's going on?" he said to Caroline Ducky.

"She's calling in the securities," said Caroline Ducky, in a new kind of English, almost without an accent. "Taking 'em from the bank."

"Christ," said Uncle Willy. "When?"

"Today's Sunday, tomorrow's Monday."

"God in Heaven," said Uncle Willy. "What a bastard she is, without telling me. That gives me sixteen hours to borrow three hundred thousand dollars. Maybe Peters just told you that to scare me."

Caroline Ducky smiled. "You too smart for what you're saying."

I had never heard anything so wonderful in my life and, although I didn't know what they were talking about, I knew I would, it was just around the corner. I suppose I was straining with the movements of body and face that have worried so many people in the years after that, because Uncle Willy realized I was in the room.

He smiled at me. "Hello, Lillian. Would you lend me three hundred thousand dollars for a month?"

I said, "You bet. If I had it, I'd . . ."

He bowed. "Thank you. Then maybe somebody else will. If they do, I'll take you fishing."

Several years before, Willy had taken my father and me and one of the big-faced men called Hatchey on his large boat and we had had a fine two days fishing in the Gulf. My pleasure in the boat had pleased Willy and there had always been talk of another trip after that. Now he left the room, patting my head as he passed me, and Caroline Ducky fell asleep by the window. I went downstairs. I heard my mother say to somebody that things would be better now that the doctor had arrived.

Walking back to my Aunt Jenny's boardinghouse, I said, "So she is having her morphine. Gets it often, I guess."

My mother stared at me. "What makes you think anything like that?"

"Caroline Ducky. Plenty makes me think plenty. Like what about all that money she's making Uncle Willy pay back because of his Cajun girl?"

"My goodness," my mother whispered. "Please don't speak that way. Please."

And I knew I had gold if I could get the coins together. But it was no use because my mother was moving her lips in prayer and that meant she had left the world for a while.

For the next few days I tried games on Jenny, hinting at the morphine, deliberately mispronouncing it, giving her pieces of the conversation between Uncle Willy and Caroline Ducky, saying that I had read in books that men often had outside women like the Cajun girl and what did she think, but I got nowhere. Jenny said we should mind our own business because rich people like my ma's family often got into muddles not meant for the rest of us.

It was a difficult time for me. I wandered about the house at night and Mrs. Caronne, Aunt Jenny's oldest boarder, complained; I wrote two poems about the pleasures of autumn love; I skipped school and spent the days sitting in front of St. Louis Cathedral and one night I wandered back-of-town and got chased home by a cop. I was, of course, at an age of half understanding the people of my world, but I was sure, as are most young people, that there were simple answers and the world, or my own limitations, were depriving me of a mathematical solution. I began, for the first time in my life, to sulk and remain silent, no longer having any faith in what I would say if I did talk, and no faith in what I would hear from anybody else. The notebooks of those days are filled with question marks: the large, funny, sad questions of the very young.

The troubles of Aunt Lily were not spoken about and my mother, as far as I know, did not return to the house. But I did, every few days, circling it, standing down the street, seeing nothing, not even Honey. But after two weeks that was unbearable and so I decided to take some pickles to Caroline Ducky. As I turned in the back entrance, Uncle Willy came out the side entrance to load his car with fishing rods and a shotgun. He looked fine and easy in old tweed clothes and good boots.

When he saw me he said, "I'm going fishing and maybe a bird or two."

"Oh," I said, "I wish I were going. I do. I do."

"I'd like to have you," he said.

It's been too many years for me to remember how long we drove on the river road, but it was a long way and I was happier — exalted was the word I used when I thought about it afterward — than I had ever been before. It was as if I had changed my life and was proud of myself for the courage of the change. The wilder the country grew, the more we bumped along on the oyster shell roads, the wilder grew my fantasies: I was a rebel leader going to Africa to arouse my defeated tribe; I was a nun on my way to a leper colony; and when a copperhead crossed the road I was one of those crazy lady dancers who wound snakes around their bodies and seduced all men. Willy and I did not speak for a very long time, not one sentence, and then he said, "Oh, Lord, what about your mama, a toothbrush, all that stuff?"

There are many ways of falling in love and one seldom is more interesting or valid than another unless, of course, one of them lasts so long that it becomes something else, like your arm or leg about which you neither judge nor protest. I was not ever to fall in love very often, but certainly this was the first time and I would like to think that I learned from it. But the mixture of ecstasy as it clashed with criticism of myself and the man was to be repeated all my life, and the only thing that made the feeling for Uncle Willy different was the pain of that first recognition: not of love, but of the struggles caused by love; the blindness of a young girl trying to make simple sexual desire into something more complex, more poetic, more unreachable.

Somewhere, after that silent time, we stopped at a small store where Uncle Willy seemed to know the old lady who was sitting on the porch. He telephoned my mother from a back room and came out to say that all was O.K. He bought me a toothbrush and a comb, a pair of boots, heavy socks, a heavy woolen shirt, and twenty-four handkerchiefs. Maybe it was the extravagance of twenty-four that made me cry.

The bayou country has changed now, and if I hadn't seen it again a few months ago I would have forgotten what it looked like, which is the measure of the strangeness of that day because I remember best what things look like and forget what it has been like to be with them. But even now I could walk the route that Willy took that day so long ago as we left the car and began to move north, sometimes on a rough path, more often through undergrowth of strange and tangled roots. Swamp oak, cypress, sent out roots above ground and small plants and fern pushed against the wild high dark green leaves of a plant I had never seen before. There was constant movement along the ground and I was sweating with fear of snakes. Once

76

Uncle Willy, ahead of me, called out and waved me away. I saw that the swamp had come in suddenly and that he was deep in the mush, pulling himself up and out by throwing his arms around a black gum tree. He was telling me to move to my left but I didn't understand what he meant until I sank into the mud, my feet, my ankles going in as if underground giants were pulling at them. I liked it, it was soft and comfortable, and I leaned down to watch the things moving around me: crawfish, flat small things the shape of salamanders, then the brownness of something the size of my hand with a tail twice as long. I don't know how long I stood there, but I know Willy had called to me several times before I saw him. Above me now he had tied a branch to his pants belt and was throwing it a foot from me. It could not have been easy for him to pull me out as he stood on uncertain ground with my dead weight at the other end. I watched the power of the shoulders and the arms with the sleepy admiration of a woman in love. I think he was puzzled by my slowness, my lack of excitement or fear, because he kept asking me if something had happened and said he had been a fool to try a shortcut to the house.

I don't know where I thought we were going, or if I thought about it at all, but the house was the meanest I had ever seen and, over the next two days, more crowded with people. There was a room with three beds, and two others of Spanish moss on the floor, a kitchen of ells and wandering corners, dirty with

77

coal smoke, filled with half-broken chairs and odd
forgotten things against the walls. Willy was as gay
as my father had always said he was, embracing people who came and went, throwing a small child in the
air, and cooing at a baby who lay in an old box. He
was at home here, this man who was accustomed to the
most immaculate of houses, the imitated eighteenth-
century elegance of Aunt Lily's house. The dirt and
mess pleased him and so did the people. I could not
sort them out, the old from the young, the relations of
the men to the women, what child belonged to whom,
but they were all noisy with pleasure at Willy's arrival, and bowls of hot water were brought from the
stove and an old woman and a young woman cleaned
his boots and washed his feet. A young girl of about
my age took my shoes to dry on the stove and gave me
a bowl and a dirty rag to wash with. I must have
drawn back from the rag — obsessive cleanliness
now seems to me less embarrassing than it seemed
that day, New Orleans being a dirty city when I was
young, with open sewers and epidemics — because
Willy said something in Cajun French and the rag
was taken out of my hand.

It was a good night, the best I had ever had up to
then. The dinner was wonderful: jambalaya, raccoon
stew, and wild duck with bitter pickles, all hot with
red pepper that made the barrel-wine necessary after
each bite. The talk was loud and everybody spoke
together except when Willy spoke, but we were deep
in Cajun country and my school French needed ad-

justment to the omitted sounds and dropped syllables. My pleasure in food and wine was, of course, my pleasure in Willy as he chased wine with whiskey, wolfed the food, and boomed and laughed and was amused, and pleased with me. I remember that a very tall man came into the room, a man in city clothes, and that my uncle left with him to sit on the porch, and everybody else disappeared. But after that I don't remember much because I was drunk and woke up in the bedroom that smelled of other people and saw two women on beds and one on the floor. I have never known whether I heard that night or the next night three quarrelsome voices outside the house, and my uncle's voice saying, "If it goes wrong, and the last one did, I'll get the blame. Nobody else. And that will be curtains." A man kept saying, "You got no choice." I had heard that voice before but I was too sleepy to think about it. Certainly by the time Willy shook me awake at dawn he was in a fine humor, laughing down in my face, saying I must never tell my mother he had got me drunk and to get ready now for the ducks.

I have been duck shooting many times since that early morning, but I have never liked it again because it never again had to do with the pleasure of crouching near Willy in the duck blind. I was then, was always to be, a bad shot and once Willy was angry with me because I ruined the flight overhead, but later he did so well and the dogs made such fine recoveries that we came back with fourteen ducks by nine o'clock. The house was empty and Willy made us giant sandwiches of many meats and peppers and said we were going to the store. We walked around to where we had left the car and drove down the bayou road to a settlement of twenty or thirty houses and a store that seemed to have everything — barrels of coffee, boots, bolts of cloth, guns, sausages, cheeses and ropes of red peppers, fur hats, oars, fish traps and dried fish.

I was standing on the porch when I heard Willy say to somebody inside, "Wait a minute, please. I'm on the phone. Certainly you can see that." Then a young man passed me carrying to our car a case of liquor, three or four giant bolts of cloth, a box of ladies' shoes with fancy buckles, a carton of coffee beans and a sewing machine. Inside, Willy said, "Hatchey, Hatchey? Ask them to hold off. No, it's not too late. Send a cable to the boat." (I don't know if I knew then the name Hatchey belonged to the man I had met on Willy's boat, and who had been outside on the porch the night before, or if I recognized it a long time later when my father told my mother about the troubles.) Then Willy came out and got in the car. The owner of the store called out about a check for last month's stuff and now all this, but Willy waved him away and said his office would send it. The owner said that would be fine, he just hoped Mr. Willy understood he needed the money, and the car drove off without me. A few minutes later it made a circle in the road and came back to the store. Willy opened the door for me and said, "Forgive me, kid. It's not a good day."

When we reached the house, Willy got out of the car and strode off. I didn't see him again until supper and then, as people thanked him for the gifts, he was bad-tempered and drank a lot. There had been plans for treeing raccoons that night, but Willy wouldn't go and wouldn't let me go. He and I sat on the porch for a long time while he drank whiskey and one of the old ladies brought pitchers of water for him. I think he had forgotten I was there because suddenly he began to whistle, a short call, then a long call. A young woman came down a side path as if she had been waiting there. She sat on the porch steps, at his feet. The second time he touched her hair I made a sound I had never heard myself make before, but neither of them noticed. A long time later, he threw an empty whiskey bottle into space, got up from his chair, toppled it as the girl rose to help him. She moved in back of him, put both arms under his, and they moved down the road. I followed them, not caring that I could almost certainly be heard as the oyster shell path crunched under me. They didn't go very far. There was another house, hidden by the trees, and then I knew I had seen the girl several times before; a big, handsome, heavy girl with fine dark hair.

I went back to the porch and sat there all night in a state that I could not describe with any truth because

I believe that what I felt that night was what I was to feel about myself and other people years later: the humiliation of vanity, the irrational feeling of rejection from a man who, of course, paid me no mind, and had no reason to do so. It is possible to feel many conflicts and not know they are conflicts when you are young: I was at one minute less than nothing and, at another, powerful enough to revenge myself with the murder of Willy. My head and body seemed not to belong together, unable to carry the burden of me. Then, as later, I revenged myself on myself: when the sun came up I left the porch, no longer fearing the swamps. On the way down the road I, who many years later was to get sick at the sight of one in a zoo, stumbled on a snake and didn't care. A few hours after that, a truck gave me a ride into New Orleans. I had been walking in the wrong direction. I did not see Willy again for five years, and if he worried about my disappearance that night, I was never to hear about it.

One July day, three or four years later, on a beach, my father said to my mother, "What's the verdict on Willy?" He was asking what my mother's family was saying.

She said, "I'm sorry for him."

"Yes," said my father, "I am sure you are, but that's not what I'm asking."

"What can they do," she said, as she always did when my father attacked her family. "It isn't their fault that he lost everything."

"Have they forbidden you to see him?"

"Now, now," said my mother.

"So they have forbidden you."

"I'll see him as my conscience dictates," said my mother, "forbid or not, but I don't want fights."

I was old enough, grown by now, to say, "What happened?"

My father said, "He sent down a shipload of guns with Hatchey Moore intended for Christmas to use. They stopped the ship. There was a scandal."

"Guns to put down the natives?"

"Yes."

"You forgive that?" I asked.

"It's always been a disgrace," said my father who, to the end of his life, was a kind of left liberal who had admiration for the capitalist victors. "But it wasn't all Willy himself. He was just acting for the company. He happened to get caught. So they fired him. That old shooting-up stuff isn't liked by the new boys. Too raw. So Willy took the rap."

"And you feel sorry for him?"

"Yes, I do," said my father, "he's stone dead broke. He was good to me."

I said, "He's a murderer."

"Oh, my! Oh, my!" said my mother. "We're all weak vessels."

During those years, because I had started to go to college, we went less often to New Orleans, three or four times, perhaps, for a month. On each visit, my mother went to see Aunt Lily, but I never again went in the front door of the house. I would go to the kitchen entrance to call on Caroline Ducky, the last time a few months before she died. She looked fine, that hot June day, more vigorous than ever. We spoke of Uncle Willy. She took for granted that I knew what everybody else knew: he had been thrown out of "the big company," had started his own fruit import company and was, according to New Orleans gossip, having a hard time. Somehow, somewhere, my aunt's money was again involved, but that made no sense to me because I couldn't see why she gave it or why he once again took it from her. But then I was a young eighteen and so little of what older people did made any sense to me that I had stopped worrying about it, finding it easier and more rewarding to understand people in books.

On one of the visits to Caroline Ducky, she said, "You ever see your Uncle Willy?"

"No."

"Me neither, much. He come around this house maybe once a month, pick up something, sleep in his office."

"Or with the Cajun girl."

"What Cajun girl? The part nigger Cajun girl?"

"I don't know," I said. "It doesn't make any difference to me if she's part nigger."

"Well," said Caroline Ducky's loud voice, "it makes a difference to me, you little white Yankee know-nothing."

I had already come half distance up the slippery

mountain dangers of liberalism. "I think maybe it's the only solution in the end. Whites and blacks . . ."

Caroline Ducky's large sewing basket went by my head. The old lady had remarkable strength, because when she saw the basket had missed me she rose and pulled me from the chair. "Get you down and pick up the mess you made."

As I was crawling around for needles and spools, fitting thimbles back into the pretty old box, she said, "That a nice box. Your mama gave it to me. I leave it to you when I go to die."

"I don't want it. I don't like people to throw things at me."

"You got a hard road to go," she said. "Part what you born from is good, part a mess of shit. Like your Aunt Lily. She made the shit and now she sit in it and poke around."

I was old enough to know what passed for wisdom among ladies: "I guess she's not had an easy time, Aunt Lily. Uncle Willy wanting her money, and his girls and all. That's what many people say."

"Many people is full a shit." With the years Caroline Ducky said shit more often than anybody I ever met except the head carpenter at the old Lyceum Theatre in Rochester, New York.

"Willy's got his side," said the old lady. "Where and why you think the morphine come here?"

I was so excited that I dropped the thread I was rewinding and tried not to shout. "The morphine the doctor gives Aunt Lily for her headaches?"

"He don't give her no morphine 'cause she don't have no headaches. Getting bad now, she won't last long." And Caroline Ducky giggled. (She was wrong. Aunt Lily lived another twenty-three years.) I guess Caroline Ducky was savoring Aunt Lily's death because she kept giggling for a while. Then she said, "That Peters ain't all nigger. His grandpa had a Wop store on Rampart Street. Wops know about stuff like that."

"Stuff like what?"

"Morphine," she screamed. "You wearing me out. And Wops make good fancy men. Peters been with your Aunt Lily long time now, but Mona Simpson down the road had him before that."

Over thirty years later, when *Toys in the Attic* had been produced and published, I had a letter from Honey. I guess he was out of the Mobile loony bin, at least for a while, because the letter had a San Diego postmark. He wanted to know if I ever came San Diego way, were my aunts still living and did I ever visit New Orleans; he himself never went there anymore although he still owned the St. Charles Avenue house, and, by the way, had I meant Mrs. Prine in my play to be his mother and her fancy man to be Peters? If I had, he didn't mind a bit, he'd just like to know. I had not realized until Honey's letter that the seeds of Mrs. Prine had, indeed, flown from Aunt Lily's famous gardenias to another kind of garden, but I thought it wise to deny even that to anybody as nutty as Honey. I showed my denial to Hammett, who talked me out of mailing it, saying that the less I had to do with Honey the better.

And that was because years before the letter, and years after that last time I ever saw Caroline Ducky, Aunt Lily and Honey, on her yearly New York buying sprees for jewelry and clothes and furniture, came twice to visit us on the farm in Pleasantville. I don't know why I invited them, some old hangover of curiosity, I guess, wanting to fill in missing parts of myself.

The first visit was O.K., although Honey seemed even more odd than I remembered and there was some mention of his nervous troubles. After they left, the cook reported that she had seen him kick our largest poodle and put a half-eaten piece of chocolate cake in his pocket.

A few years later Aunt Lily and Honey drove out with my father on a Sunday morning. Honey and I went swimming and I showed him the stables, where he teased a bad-tempered pony who kicked him. At lunch the conversation was disjointed. My aunt, as usual, ate almost nothing, but Honey went four times to the buffet table.

My father said, "You have a good capacity, Honey. The fish is pretty good, but how can you eat that other junk?"

"That other junk," I said, "is sauerbraten. I cooked it for the first time, to please you. It's German and I thought you'd like it."

"It can't be German," said my father, "it's Jewish.

I don't know where you learned to make bad Jewish food."

When Dash laughed I was about to say something about loyalty, but was interrupted by Aunt Lily, who said to Honey, "Go vomit, dear."

Honey said, "I don't want to."

Aunt Lily sighed. Then she turned to my father. "You still see my husband, so called?"

"I'd like to see Willy, but I don't get home much anymore, and Willy doesn't come to New York."

"Oh, yes, he does," said Aunt Lily, "he comes all the time. He just doesn't want to see you anymore. He has no loyalty to anybody."

My father's face was angry. "He doesn't come North and you know it, because he doesn't have any money. None."

"That's right," said Honey through a mouthful of something. "Mama took it all. It's for me, she says, but she gives a lot to Peters."

Aunt Lily seemed to be dozing, so Honey said it again. When he got no answer he said it the third time and added, "That's because of fucking."

My father laughed. "Remember, Honey, my daughter is in the room." Then he said to Dash, "Some nuts." And he got up from the table to get himself a piece of sauerbraten.

Dash said to me, "Your father who hates the stuff has now eaten four pieces of it."

"You have to try everything to know you don't like it," said my father.

Aunt Lily turned to Honey. "I don't like your talk. Shut your face."

My father said to Aunt Lily, "Never punish a child for telling the truth. Haven't I lived by that, Lillian?"

"And by much else," I said.

My father turned to Dash. "Lillian's got the disposition of her mother's family. My family were good-natured. Look what's happening to Honey."

Honey had gone out into the hallway and was standing on his head. Aunt Lily said, "It's his way of adjusting his stomach. The doctor told me Willy has syphilis."

"Oh, Christ," my father said to me, "any time your mother's family get stuck with anything, crazy children, bad stocks and bonds, other people gave them syphilis."

I said to Aunt Lily, "I don't believe you. Uncle Willy is a fine man. I admire him very much."

Dash said, "Watch it, you're not going to like what you're saying."

Soon after lunch, Aunt Lily said she wanted "a lie-down," was there a room to rest in. I took her upstairs, Dash went to his room, my father and I sat reading, and once in a while I watched from the window to see that Honey was doing nothing more than dozing on the lawn. Toward four o'clock their car arrived and I went to tell Aunt Lily. There was no answer to my knocks, but when I opened the door Aunt Lily was not asleep: she was sitting in a chair, staring out the window at the top of a tree. I spoke to her several times, moved in front of her, leaned over her. There was no sign of recognition, no answer. I went to get Honey. He was sitting in the car. Before I spoke he said, "She gets like that."

"What's the matter with her?"

"Peters takes care of it, not me. I'll send him back tomorrow."

"Where are you going?"

"To New York. I got a date."

I said to the chauffeur, "Wait here, please. This gentleman can't pay for the car without his mother," and went off to find Hammett. He put down his book and went with me to the room where Aunt Lily was sitting. He pulled a chair up next to her.

"You're a very handsome man," she said. "Handsome people have an easier time in this vale of tears."

"Your car is waiting," he said.

"I hope you are good to my niece. Are you good to . . ." and faltered over my name.

"Better than she deserves," said Dash. "Please get up. I will help you to the car."

"In our South," she said, "it is a mark of woman's trust when she allows the use of her first name. Call me Lily."

"No," he said, "one is enough," and reaching down for her arms he brought her to her feet. But he had not correctly gauged her humor, because she pulled sharply away from him, moved to the bureau, and held tight to its sides.

I think she saw me for the first time. She said, "What are you doing here? You like Willy. You're no good."

"We'll talk about that another day," Dash said and moved quickly to take away the alligator pocketbook that had been her reason for the move to the bureau.

"Give me my bag immediately," she said, "there's a great deal of jewelry in that bag."

Dash laughed. "More than jewelry. Come along."

I followed them down the stairs and stood on the porch as Dash moved her down the driveway to the car. Once she stumbled and, as he caught her, she threw off his arm and moved away with the overdignified motions of a drunk. As Dash shut the door of the car, I heard Honey laugh and he waved to me as they drove past the porch.

"Well," said Dash, "that will be enough of them, I hope."

"What was that about her pocketbook?"

"She wanted a fix. I don't know what kind and don't want to. A bad pair. Why don't you leave them alone?"

"What did you mean when I said Uncle Willy was a fine man and you said I wasn't going to like what I was saying?"

"You told me that even as a child you hated what his company was doing, the murders, and what it meant to you."

"I never told you Willy did the murders. He's a

good man. He just went where life took him, I guess."

"Oh, sure. Now let's leave that talk for another day or forever."

"Why should we leave it? You always say that when . . ."

"Because I want to leave it," he said, "maybe in the hope you'll find out for yourself."

I thought about that for a few days, sulked with it, then left it and forgot about it.

A year later Dash and I moved to Hollywood for four or five months, each of us to write a movie. Soon after we got there, we had one of our many partings: Hammett was drinking heavily, dangerously. I was sick of him and myself and so one weekend I took off to see my aunts in New Orleans. I would not have liked to live with them for very long, but for a few days I always liked their modest, disciplined life in the shabby little house that was all they could afford since each had stopped working. It was nice, after the plush of Hollywood, to sleep on a cot in the ugly living room, crowded with stuff that poor people can't bring themselves to throw away, nice to talk about what we would have for the good dinner to which one of many old ladies would be invited to show off my aunts' quiet pride in me. Nicest of all was to take a small piece of all the Hollywood money and buy them new winter coats and dresses at Maison Blanche, to be delivered after I left for fear that they'd make me return them if I were there, and then to go along to Solari's, the fine grocers, and load a taxi with delicacies they liked and would never buy, hear Jenny protest over the calves'-foot jelly she liked so much and watch Hannah's lovely, greedy eyes deny the words she made over the cans of giant Belgian asparagus.

The taxi driver and I were piling in the Solari cartons when I saw Willy staring at me from across the street. He was much older: the large body hung now with loose flesh, the hair was tumbled, the heavy face lined and colored sick. I crossed the street and kissed him. He put an arm around me and pressed my head to his shoulder.

He said very softly, "So you turned into a writer? Come and have lunch with me."

He paid the taxi driver to take the stuff to my aunts' house and we walked a few blocks to Decatur Street and turned into an old building facing the river that had a large sign saying, "Guacosta Fruit Import Company." As we went up the steps he said, "This is my company, I am rich again. Do you need anything money can buy?"

Directly opposite the stair landing was an enormous room entirely filled by a dining room table. Along the table, at intervals of ten or twelve chairs, were printed signs, "French," "Mexican," "German," "Creole," "Plain steaks, chops," and seated at the table, sometimes in groups of four or five, occasionally alone, were perhaps twenty men who looked like, and maybe were, the men I had seen at Willy's house on the Sundays so many years before.

Willy put his arm around me, "What kind of food,

kid? There's a different good chef for each kind."
When I chose Creole, he whispered to the two men
who were sitting in that section and they rose and
moved down the table. We must have had a lot of
wine because our lunch lasted long after everybody
left and I didn't get back to my aunts until six that
evening, and then I was so rocky that I had a hard
time convincing them not to send for a doctor and
during the night, through the thin walls, I heard them
talking, and twice Hannah came to turn on the light
and look down at me.

I was in the shower the next morning when there
was a knock on the bathroom door and Willy said,
"Come along. We're going to the country."

Going down the steps, I saw my aunts in the garden.
I called out and Hannah waved, but Jenny turned her
back, and Hannah dropped her hand.

Toward midday we went through the town of Hammond and Willy said, "In a few minutes." The long
driveway, lined with moss oak, ended at a galleried
plantation house. "We're home," he said. It was a
beautiful, half empty house of oval rooms and delicate colors. Beyond the great lawns were strawberry
fields and, in the distance, ten or twelve horses moved
slowly in a field.

I said, "I like my farm in Pleasantville. But there's
nothing like the look of Southern land, or there's no
way for me to get over thinking so. It's home for me
still."

"I'll give you this place," he said. "I'd like you to
have it."

Late in the afternoon, after a long walk in the straw-berry acres, I said my aunts would be hurt if I didn't have dinner with them. We had an argument about that, and then we started back to New Orleans. Willy's driving was erratic and I realized that he had had a great deal to drink during the day. When we took a swerve I saw that he had been dozing at the wheel. He stopped the car, said he thought I should drive, and he slept all the way to the outskirts of New Orleans.

I hadn't expected the voice, nor the soberness with which he said, "Pull over for a minute."

We stopped in the flat land that was beginning then to be as ugly as it is now.

"Whcn are you going to Los Angeles?"

"Tomorrow morning."

"Do you have to?"

"No. I don't have to do anything," believing, as I had done all my life that was true, or believing it for the minute I said it.

"I've been faking. I'm broke, more than I've ever been. Stone broke. That lovely house will have to go this week, I guess, and I haven't got the stuff to pay a month's rent on the office. I owe everybody from here to Memphis to Costa Rica."

"I have some money now," I said.

"Don't do that," he said sharply, "don't say it again." He got out of the car, walked around it and came to my window. His face was gay and he was grinning now. "I am going to Central America on Friday. I'll move the way I first went as a boy, on mules. I'm the best banana buyer in the world. I'll get all the credit I want when I get there, San José, Cartago. Three or four months. I can't tell you how I want to go the way I did when I was young. It's rough country and wonderful. Come with me. You'll see with me what you could never see without me. A mule hurts, at first, but if I were your age . . ." He touched my hand. "Anyway it's time you and I finished what we have already started. Come on."

That night, at dinner, I told my aunts I would not be leaving them until Friday. Hannah was pleased but Jenny said nothing. The next morning when I went into the dining room, Jenny pointed to a large florist box and watched me unwrap a dozen orchid sprays. She said Willy had phoned and left the name of a man who made fine riding boots, he had ordered me two pairs and I was to go down immediately, fit them, and come to his office for lunch. I was uneasy at the expression on Jenny's face and went to get dressed. When I came back she was sitting in the hall opposite my door, Hannah standing next to her. She raised her hand and Hannah disappeared.

"You're going riding on a horse?"

"Yes," I said.

"As I remember your riding, you don't need made-to-order boots."

"I'm going to Central America for a few months."

Jenny had rheumatism and always moved with difficulty. Now she got out of the chair, holding to a table. When I moved to help her she pulled her arm away from me.

"In that case," she said, "you can't stay here. You have been our child, maybe more, but you can't stay here."

I said, "Jenny! Jenny!" But she pushed passed me and slammed the door of the kitchen.

I lay on the bed for a long time but after a while I packed my bags and went to find a taxicab. It was raining a little and they were scarce that day and by the time I reached St. Charles Avenue there was a sudden, frightening curtain of rain, so common in New Orleans. I went into a restaurant and had a drink.

I phoned the Beverly Hills house from the restaurant. I said to Hammett, "I'm in New Orleans. I'm not coming back to Hollywood for a while and I didn't want you to worry."

"How are you?" he said.

"O.K. and you?"

"I'm O.K. I miss you."

"I miss you, too. Is there a lady in my bedroom?"

He laughed. "I don't think so, but they come and go. Except you. You just go."

"I had good reason," I said.

"Yes," he said, "you did."

"Anyway," I said, "I'll be back in a few months. Take care of yourself and I'll call you when I come back. Maybe then we won't have to talk about reasons and can just have a nice dinner."

"No," he said, "I don't think so. I'm not crazy about women who sleep with murderers."

"I haven't slept with him. And he's never killed anybody."

"No," he said, "he just hired people to do it for him. I was in that racket for a lot of years and I don't like it." He sighed. "Do what you want. Have a nice time but don't call me."

I flew to Los Angeles that night. I didn't telephone Dash but somebody must have told him I was there because after about ten days he called me, said he was on the wagon, and we had a nice dinner together. I never saw Willy again and never had an answer to the letter I had mailed from New Orleans.

On my birthday that year my aunts sent a hand-knitted sweater and the usual box of pralines with a note saying all the usual affectionate things and adding, as a postscript, that Willy had gone into bankruptcy and barely avoided jail for reasons they couldn't figure out. And not many months after that I had a telephone call from a man I knew who worked on a New Orleans newspaper. He said that Willy, driving up the road to Hammond and the strawberry plantation, with two men, had had an automobile accident that killed everybody in the car, and did I want to comment for the obit.

Years later, Caroline Ducky's grandchild, who had worked for Willy as a cleaning woman, said it hadn't been any mystery, that accident, because he had started out dead drunk from a one-room, cockroach apartment he had rented on Bourbon Street.

JULIA

I HAVE here changed most of the names. I don't know that it matters anymore, but I believe the heavy girl on the train still lives in Cologne and I am not sure that even now the Germans like their premature anti-Nazis. More important, Julia's mother is still living and so, perhaps, is Julia's daughter. Almost certainly, the daughter's father lives in San Francisco.

In 1937, after I had written *The Children's Hour* and *Days to Come,* I had an invitation to attend a theatre festival in Moscow. Whenever in the past I wrote about that journey, I omitted the story of my trip through Berlin because I did not feel able to write about Julia.

Dorothy Parker and her husband, Alan Campbell, were going to Europe that same August, and so we crossed together on the old *Normandie,* a pleasant trip even though Campbell, and his pretend-good-natured feminine jibes, had always made me uneasy.

When we reached Paris I was still undecided about going on to Moscow. I stayed around, happy to meet Gerald and Sara Murphy for the first time, Hemingway, who came up from Spain, and James Lardner, Ring Lardner's son, who was soon to enlist in the International Brigade and to lose his life in Spain a few months later.

I liked the Murphys. I was always to like and be interested in them, but they were not for me what they had been to an older generation. They were, possibly, all that Calvin Tomkins says in his biography: they had style, Gerald had wit, Sara grace and shrewdness, and that summer, soon after they had lost both their sons, they had a sweet dignity. But through the many years I was to see them after that I came to believe they were not as bonny as others thought them, or without troubles with each other, and long before the end — the end of my knowing them, I mean, a few years before Gerald died, when they saw very few of their old friends — I came to think that too much of their lives had been based on style. Style is mighty pleasant for those who benefit from it, but maybe not always rewarding for those who make and live by its necessarily strict rules.

There were many other people that summer in

Paris, famous and rich, who invited Dottie for dinners and country lunches and the tennis she didn't play and the pools she didn't swim in. It gave me pleasure then, and forever after, that people courted her. I was amused at her excessive good manners, a kind of put-on, often there to hide contempt and dislike for those who flattered her at the very minute she begged for the flattery. When she had enough to drink the good manners got so good they got silly, but then the words came funny and sharp to show herself, and me, I think, that nobody could buy her. She was wrong: they could and did buy her for years. But they only bought a limited ticket to her life and in the end she died on her own road.

It was a new world for me. I had been courted around New York and Hollywood, as is everybody who has been a success in the theatre and young enough not to have been too much on display. But my invitations were second-class stuff compared to Dottie's admirers that month in Paris. I had a fine time, one of the best of my life. But one day, after a heavy night's drinking, I didn't anymore. I was a child of the Depression, a kind of Puritan Socialist, I guess — although to give it a name is to give it a sharper outline than it had — and I was full of the strong feelings the early Roosevelt period brought to many people. Dottie had the same strong feelings about something we all thought of as society and the future, but the difference between us was more than generational — she was long accustomed to much I didn't want. It

was true that she always turned against the famous
and the rich who attracted her, but I never liked
them well enough to bother that much.

I had several times that month spoken on the phone
with my beloved childhood friend Julia, who was
studying medicine in Vienna, and so the morning
after the heavy drinking I called Julia to say I would
come to Vienna the next day en route to Moscow. But
that same night, very late, she called back.

She said, "I have something important for you to
do. Maybe you'll do it, maybe you can't. But please
stay in Paris for a few days and a friend will come to
see you. If things work as I hope, you'll decide to go
straight to Moscow by way of Berlin and I'll meet you
on your way back."

When I said I didn't understand, who was the
friend, why Berlin, she said, "I can't answer questions. Get a German visa tomorrow. You'll make your
own choice, but don't talk about it now."

It would not have occurred to me to ignore what
Julia told me to do because that's the way it had always been between us. So I went around the next
morning to the German consulate for a visa. The
consul said they'd give me a traveling permit, but
would not allow me to stay in Berlin overnight, and
the Russian consul said that wasn't unusual for people
en route to Moscow.

I waited for two days and was about to call Julia
again on the day of the morning I went down for an
early breakfast in the dining room of the Hotel Meu-

rice. (I had been avoiding Dottie and Alan, all invitations, and was troubled and annoyed by two snippy, suspicious notes from Alan about what was I up to, why was I locked in my room?) The concierge said the gentleman on the bench was waiting for me. A tall middle-aged man got up from the bench and said, "Madame Hellman? I come to deliver your tickets and to talk with you about your plans. Miss Julia asked me to call with the travel folders."

We went into the dining room, and when I asked him what he would like he said, in German, "Do you think I can have an egg, hot milk, a roll? I cannot pay for them."

When the waiter moved away, the tall man said, "You must not understand German again. I made a mistake."

I said I didn't understand enough German to worry anybody, but he didn't answer me and took to reading the travel folders until the food came. Then he ate very fast, smiling as he did it, as if he were remembering something pleasant from a long ago past. When he finished, he handed me a note. The note said, "This is my friend, Johann. He will tell you. But *I* tell you, don't push yourself. If you can't you can't, no dishonor. Whatever, I will meet you soon. Love, Julia."

Mr. Johann said, "I thank you for fine breakfast. Could we walk now in Tuileries?"

As we entered the gardens he asked me how much I knew about Benjamin Franklin, was I an expert? I said I knew almost nothing. He said he admired Franklin and perhaps someday I could find him a nice photograph of Franklin in America. He sat down suddenly on a bench and mopped his forehead on this cool, damp day.

"Have you procured a German visa?"

"A traveling visa. I cannot stay overnight. I can only change stations in Berlin for Moscow."

"Would you carry for us fifty thousand dollars? We think, we do not guarantee, you will be without trouble. You will be taking the money to enable us to bribe out many already in prison, many who soon will be. We are a small group, valuable workers against Hitler. We are of no common belief or religion. The people who will meet you for the money, if your consent is given, were once small publishers. We are of Catholic, Communist, many beliefs. Julia has said that I must remind you for her that you are afraid of being afraid, and so will do what sometimes you cannot do, and that could be dangerous to you and to us."

I took to fiddling with things in my pocketbook, lit a cigarette, fiddled some more. He sat back as if he were very tired, and stretched.

After a while I said, "Let's go and have a drink."

He said, "I repeat. We think all will go well, but much could go wrong. Julia says I must tell you that, but that if we should not hear from you by the time of Warsaw, Julia will use her family with the American ambassador there through Uncle John."

"I know her family. There was a time she didn't believe in them much."

"She said you would note that. And so to tell you that her Uncle John is now governor. He does not like her but did not refuse her money for his career. And that her mother's last divorce has made her mother dependent on Julia as well."

I laughed at this picture of Julia controlling members of her very rich family. I don't think we had seen each other more than ten or twelve times since we were eighteen years old and so the years had evidently brought changes I didn't know about. Julia had left college, gone to Oxford, moved on to medical school in Vienna, had become a patient-pupil of Freud's. We had once, in the last ten years, spent a Christmas holiday together, and one summer, off Massachusetts, we had sailed for a month on her small boat, but in the many letters we had written in those years neither of us knew much more than the bare terms of each other's life, nothing of the daily stuff that is the real truth, the importance.

I knew, for example, that she had become, maybe always was, a Socialist, and lived by it, in a one-room apartment in a slum district of Vienna, sharing her great fortune with whoever needed it. She allowed herself very little, wanted very little. Oddly, gifts to me did not come into the denial: they were many and extravagant. Through the years, whenever she saw anything I might like, it was sent to me: old Wedgwood pieces, a Toulouse-Lautrec drawing, a fur-lined coat we saw together in Paris, a set of Balzac that she put in a rare Empire desk, and a wonderful set of Georgian jewelry, I think the last thing she could have had time to buy.

I said to the gray man, "Could I think it over for a few hours? That's what Julia meant."

He said, "Do not think hard. It is best not to be too prepared for matters of this kind. I will be at the station tomorrow morning. If you agree to carry the money, you will say hello to me. If you have decided it is not right for you, pass by me. Do not worry whichever is decided by you." He held out his hand, bowed, and moved away from me across the gardens.

I spent the day in and around Sainte-Chapelle, tried to eat lunch and dinner, couldn't, and went back to the hotel to pack only after I was sure Dottie and Alan would have gone to dinner with the Murphys. I left a note for them saying I was leaving early in the morning and would find them again after Moscow. I knew I had spent the whole day in a mess of indecision. Now I lay down, determined that I would not sleep until I had taken stock of myself. But decisions, particularly important ones, have always made me sleepy, perhaps because I know that I will have to make them by instinct, and thinking things out is only what other people tell me I should do. In any case, I slept through the night and rose only in time to hurry for the early morning train.

I was not pleased to find Dottie and Alan in the lobby, waiting to take me to the station. My protests were so firm and so awkward that Alan, who had a remarkable nose for deception, asked if I had a reason for not wanting them to come with me. When he went to get a taxi, I said to Dottie, "Sorry if I sounded rude. Alan makes me nervous."

She smiled, "Dear Lilly, you'd be a psychotic if he didn't."

At the railroad station I urged them to leave me when my baggage was carried on, but something had excited Alan: perhaps my nervousness; certainly not his claim that they had never before known anybody who was en route to Moscow. He was full of bad jokes about what I must not say to Russian actors, how to smuggle out caviar, and all the junk people like Alan say when they want to say something else.

I saw the gray man come down the platform. As he came near us Alan said, "Isn't that the man I saw you with in the Tuileries yesterday?" And as I turned to say something to Alan, God knows what it would have been, the gray man went past me and was moving back into the station.

I ran toward him. "Mr. Johann. Please, Mr. Johann." As he turned, I lost my head and screamed, "Please don't go away. *Please.*"

He stood still for what seemed like a long time, frowning. Then he moved slowly back toward me, as if he were coming with caution, hesitation.

Then I remembered: I said, "I only wanted to say hello. Hello to you, Mr. Johann, hello."

"Hello, Madame Hellman."

Alan had come to stand near us. Some warning had to be made. "This is Mr. Campbell and Miss Parker there. Mr. Campbell says he saw us yesterday and now he will ask me who you are and say that he didn't know we knew each other so well that you would come all this way to say goodbye to me."

Mr. Johann said, without hesitation, "I wish I could say that was true. But I have come to search for my nephew who is en route to Poland. He is not in his coach, he is late, as is his habit. His name is W. Franz, car 4, second class, and if I do not find him I would be most grateful if you say to him I came." He lifted his hat. "I am most glad, Madame Hellman, that we had this chance to say hello."

"Oh, yes," I said, "indeed. Hello. Hello."

When he was gone, Alan said, "What funny talk. You're talking like a foreigner."

"Sorry," I said, "sorry not to speak as well as you do in Virginia."

Dottie laughed, I kissed her and jumped for the train. I was nervous and went in the wrong direction. By the time a conductor told me where my compartment was, the train had left the station. On the connecting platform, before I reached my coach, a young man was standing holding a valise and packages. He said, "I am W. Franz, nephew, car 4, second class. This is a birthday present from Miss Julia." He handed me a box of candy and a hatbox marked "Madame Pauline." Then he bowed and moved off.

I carried the boxes to my compartment, where

two young women were sitting on the left bench. One girl was small and thin and carried a cane. The other was a big-boned woman of about twenty-eight, in a heavy coat, wrapped tight against this mild day. I smiled at them, they nodded, and I sat down. I put my packages next to me and only then noticed that there was a note pasted on the hatbox. I was frightened of it, thought about taking it to the ladies' room, decided that would look suspicious, and opened it. I had a good memory in those days for poems, for what people said, for the looks of things, but it has long since been blurred by time. But I still remember every word of that note: "At the border, leave the candy box on the seat. Open this box and wear the hat. There is no thanks for what you will do for them. No thanks from me either. But there is the love I have for you. Julia."

I sat for a long time holding the note. I was in a state that I have known since I was old enough to know myself, and that to this day frightens me and makes me unable even to move my hands. I do not mean to be foolishly modest about my intelligence: it is often high, but I have known since childhood that faced with a certain kind of simple problem, I sometimes make it so complex that there is no way out. I simply do not see what another mind grasps immediately. I was there now. Julia had not told me where to open the hatbox. To take it into the corridor or toilet might make the two ladies opposite me suspicious. And so I sat doing nothing for a long time until I realized that I didn't know when we crossed the border — a few minutes or a few hours. A decision had to be made but I could not make it.

Childhood is less clear to me than to many people: when it ended I turned my face away from it for no reason that I know about, certainly without the usual reason of unhappy memories. For many years that worried me, but then I discovered that the tales of former children are seldom to be trusted. Some people supply too many past victories or pleasures with which to comfort themselves, and other people cling to pains, real and imagined, to excuse what they have become.

I think I have always known about my memory: I know when it is to be trusted and when some dream or fantasy entered on the life, and the dream, the need of dream, led to distortion of what happened. And so I knew early that the rampage angers of an only child were distorted nightmares of reality. But I trust absolutely what I remember about Julia.

Now, so many years later, I could climb the steps without a light, move in the night through the crowded rooms of her grandparents' great Fifth Avenue house with the endless chic-shabby rooms, their walls covered with pictures, their tables crowded with objects whose value I didn't know. True, I cannot remember anything said or done in that house except for the first night I was allowed to sleep there. Julia and I were both twelve years old that New Year's Eve night, sitting at a late dinner, with courses of fish and meats, and sherbets in between to change the tastes, "clear the palate" is what her grandmother said, with watered wine for us, and red and white wine and champagne for the two old people. (Were they old? I don't know: they were her grandparents.) I cannot remember any talk at the table, but after dinner we were allowed to go with them to the music room. A servant had already set the phonograph for "So Sheep May Safely Graze," and all four of us listened until Julia rose, kissed the hand of her grandmother, the brow of her grandfather, and left the room, motioning for me to follow. It was an odd ritual, the whole thing, I thought, the life of the very rich, and beyond my understanding.

Each New Year's Eve of my life has brought back the memory of that night. Julia and I lay in twin beds and she recited odds and ends of poetry — every once in a while she would stop and ask me to recite, but I didn't know anything — Dante in Italian, Heine in German, and even though I could not understand either language, the sounds were so lovely that I felt a sweet sadness as if much was ahead in the world, much that was going to be fine and fulfilling if I could ever find my way. I did recite Mother Goose and she did Donne's "Julia," and laughed with pleasure "at his tribute to me." I was ashamed to ask if it was a joke.

Very late she turned her head away for sleep, but I said, "More, Julia, please. Do you know more?" And she turned on the light again and recited from Ovid and Catullus, names to me without countries.

I don't know when I stopped listening to look at the lovely face propped against the pillow — the lamp throwing fine lights on the thick dark hair. I cannot say now that I knew or had ever used the words gentle or delicate or strong, but I did think that night that it was the most beautiful face I had ever seen. In later years I never thought about how she looked, although when we were grown other people often said she was a "strange beauty," she "looked like nobody else," and one show-off said a "Burne-Jones face" when, of course, her face had nothing to do with Burne-Jones or fake spirituality.

There were many years, almost twenty, between that New Year's Eve and the train moving into Germany. In those years, and the years after Julia's death, I have had plenty of time to think about the love I had for her, too strong and too complicated to be defined as only the sexual yearnings of one girl for another. And yet certainly that was there. I don't know, I never cared, and it is now an aimless guessing game. It doesn't prove much that we never kissed each other; even when I leaned down in a London funeral parlor to kiss the battered face that had been so hideously put back together, it was not the awful scars that worried me: because I had never kissed her I thought perhaps she would not want it and so I touched the face instead.

A few years after that childhood New Year's Eve,
I was moved to a public school. (My father was having a bad time and couldn't afford to pay for me anymore.) But Julia and I saw each other almost every
day and every Saturday night I still slept in her grandparents' house. But, in time, our lives did change:
Julia began to travel all summer and in winter holi-
days, and when she returned all my questions about
the beauties of Europe would be shrugged off with
badly photographed snapshots of things that interested her: two blind children in Cairo — she explained that the filth carried by flies caused the blindness; people drinking from sewers in Teheran; no
St. Mark's but the miserable hovel of a gondolier in
Venice; no news of the glories of Vatican art but
stories about the poverty of Trastevere.

Once she returned with a framed photograph of a
beautiful woman who was her mother and an English-
man who was her mother's husband. I asked her what
she felt about seeing her mother — in all the years I
had never heard her mention her mother — and she
stared at me and said that her mother owned a "very
fancy castle" and the new husband poured drinks for
all the titles who liked the free stuff, but there was
also mention of Evelyn Waugh and H. G. Wells and
Nancy Cunard, and when I wanted news of them she
said she didn't know anything about them, they'd
said hello to her and that she had only wanted to get
out of the way and go to her room.

"But I didn't have a *room*," she said. "Everybody

has a suite, and there are fourteen servants somewhere below the earth, and only some of them have a window in the cell my mother calls their room, and there's only one stinking bath for all of them. My mother learns fast, wherever she is. She does not offend the host country."

Once, when we were about sixteen, we went with her grandparents at Easter time to their Adirondacks lodge, as large and shabby as was every place they lived in. Both old people drank a good deal — I think they always had, but I had only begun to notice it — and napped after every meal. But they stayed awake late into the night doing intricate picture puzzles imported from France, on two tables, and gave each other large checks for the one who finished first.

I don't remember that Julia asked their permission for our camping trips — several times we stayed away for weekends — on or near Lake Champlain. It wasn't proper camping, although we carried blankets and clean socks and dry shoes and canned food. We walked a great deal, often I fished for trout, and once, climbing a high hill, Julia threw a net over a rabbit, running with a grace and speed I had never before seen in a girl, and she showed me how to skin the rabbit. We cooked it that night wrapped in bacon and it is still among the best things I ever ate, maybe because *Robinson Crusoe* is one of the best books I ever read. Even now, seeing any island, I am busy with that rabbit and fantasies of how I would make do alone, without shelter or tools.

When we walked or fished we seldom did it side by side: that was her choice and I admired it because I believed she was thinking stuff I couldn't understand and mustn't interfere with, and maybe because I knew even then she didn't want to be side by side with anybody.

At night, wrapped in our blankets, the fire between us, we would talk. More accurately, I would ask questions and she would talk: she was one of the few people I have ever met who could give information without giving a lecture. How young it sounds now that although I had heard the name of Freud, I never knew exactly what he wrote until she told me; that Karl Marx and Engels became men with theories, instead of that one sentence in my school book which mentioned the Manifesto. But we also talked like all young people, of possible beaux and husbands and babies, and heredity versus environment, and can romantic love last, mixing stuff like that in speeches made only for the pleasure of girls on the edge of growing up.

One night, when we had been silent for a long time because she was leaning on an elbow, close to the fire, reading a German grammar, I laughed at the sounds coming from her mouth as she repeated the sentences.

She said, "No, you don't understand. People are either teachers or students. You are a student."

"Am I a good one?"

"When you find what you want, you will be very good."

I reached out and touched her hand. "I love you,

Julia." She stared at me and took my hand to her face.

It was in our nineteenth year that she went away to Oxford. The second year she was there I went to visit her. There are women who reach a perfect time of life, when the face will never again be as good, the body never as graceful or as powerful. It had happened that year to Julia, but she was no more conscious of it than she had been of being a beautiful child. Her clothes were ugly now, loose, tacky, and the shoes looked as if they had been stolen from an old man. Nobody came to her rooms because, as one smitten young Indian gentleman told me, she never asked anybody. She was invited everywhere in Oxford and in London, but the only names I remember her speaking of with respect were J. D. Bernal and J. B. S. Haldane. Once or twice we went up to the theatre in London, but she would sigh halfway through and say she had no feeling for the theatre, only Shakespeare on the page, and sometimes not even then.

The following year she wrote to tell me that she was leaving England for medical school in Vienna, with the probably vain hope that Freud would someday accept her as a student.

I wrote a number of letters that year, but the only time I heard from Julia was a cable on my birthday, followed by the Toulouse-Lautrec drawing that hangs today in my house. I was pleased that she thought I knew the excellence of Toulouse-Lautrec, because I didn't, and had to be told about him by a fellow student who used to buy me hamburgers in order, I think, to tell me about his homosexual experiences. (He was a very decorated hero during the Second World War and was killed a week before it ended.)

A few months later I had a letter from Anne-Marie Travers, a girl whom Julia and I had both known in school, but I knew better because we had gone to the same dreadful summer camp. Anne-Marie was an intelligent girl, flirtatious, good-mannered with that kind of outward early-learned passive quality that in women so often hides anger. Now, it seemed, she was in or near Vienna and her unexpected letter — I don't think we had seen each other for four or five years — said she had bumped into Julia on the street and been "snubbed," had heard from people that Julia was leading a strange life, very political, pretending not to be rich and living in the Floridsdorf district, the Socialist working-class "slums." Julia ranked second in the medical school, she had been told, the first candidate being an American also but of a German inheritance, a very remarkable boy from San Francisco, handsome in the Norwegian way, she, Anne-Marie, didn't like. It took knowing Anne-Marie to realize that German and Norwegian used in the same sentence was a combination of put-down and admiration. Anne-Marie added that her brother Sammy had recently tried to kill himself, and was I still torn between being a writer or an architect? There was something strange about the letter, some reason, some tone I didn't understand, didn't like. Then I forgot it for a month or so until her brother Sammy rang to ask me for dinner, saying that he had been living in Elba and thinking of me. He said it again at dinner, having had four whiskeys with beer chasers, and asked me if I was a virgin. This was not like Sammy, who had no interest in me, and I sensed something was to follow. At about four in the morning when we were sitting in Small's in Harlem, and there had been many more whiskeys and beers, he asked me why I had got a divorce, why hadn't I married his older brother Eliot, whose rich Detroit wife had lost all her money in the Depression, and so Eliot was again open to bids and would be right for me, although he himself thought Eliot a handsome bore. He said he rather liked his sister Anne-Marie, because he had slept with her when she was sixteen and he was eighteen. Then, perhaps because I made a sound, he said who the hell was I to talk, everybody knew about Julia and me.

It is one of the strange American changes in custom that the drunks of my day often hit each other, but never in the kind of bar fight that so often happens now with knives. In those days somebody hit somebody, and when that was finished one of them offered his hand and it would have been unheard of to refuse. (James Thurber had once thrown a glass of whiskey at me in the famous Tony's speakeasy, Hammett had pushed Thurber against a wall, Thurber had picked up a glass from another table and, in an attempt to throw it at Dash, missed and hit the waiter who was Tony's cousin. Tony called the police, saying over and over again that he had had enough of Thurber

120

through the years. Almost everybody agreed with Tony, but when the police came we were shocked and went down to the police station to say nothing had happened except a drunken accident of a broken glass; and while I don't think Thurber liked me afterward, I don't think he had liked me before. In any case, none of us ever mentioned it again.) And so, at that minute at the table at Small's, there seemed to me nothing odd about what I did. I leaned across the table, slapped Sammy in the face, got up, turned over the table, and went home. The next day a girl called me to say that Sammy couldn't remember what he had said but he was sorry, anyway, and a large amount of flowers arrived that evening. The girl called again a few days later: I said there were no hard feelings, but Sammy was a bigger dope at twenty-five than he had been at seventeen. She said she'd tell him that.

I wrote to Anne-Marie saying that whatever Julia thought or did was bound to be interesting, and that I didn't want to hear attacks on her beliefs or her life. My letter was returned, unopened or resealed, and it was to be another year before I knew why.

Not long after, I had a letter from Julia suggesting that I come to Vienna for a visit, that Freud had accepted her, that there were things I ought to learn about "the holocaust that is on its way." I wrote back that I was living with Hammett, didn't want to leave, but would come maybe next year. Subsequent letters from her talked of Hitler, Jews, radicals, Mussolini.

We wrote a great deal that year, 1933–1934, and I told her that I was trying to write a play, hadn't much hope about it, but that Hammett was pulling me along. I asked her if she liked *The Children's Hour* as a title and was hurt when she forgot the question in her next letter, which was angry with news of the armed political groups in Austria, the threat of Hitler, "the criminal guilt of the English and French in not recognizing the dangers of Fascism, German style, the other one is a peacock." There was much in her letter I didn't understand, although all of us by that time knew that the Nazis would affect our lives.

I could not write a history of those years as it seemed to us then. Or, more accurately, I could not write my own: I have no records and I do not know when I understood what. I know that Hitler — Mussolini might have escaped our notice as no more than a big-talking man in silly uniforms — had shaken many of us into radicalism, or something we called radicalism, and that our raw, new convictions would, in time, bring schisms and ugly fights. But in the early Thirties I don't believe the people I knew had done much more than sign protests, listen to the shocking stories of the few German émigrés who had come to New York or Hollywood, and given money to one cause or another. We were disturbed by the anti-Semitism that was an old story in Germany and some of us had sense enough to see it as more than that. Many people thought of it as not much more than the ignorant rantings of a house painter and his low-down friends, who would certainly be rejected by the Germans, who were for my generation an "advanced," "cultivated" people.

But by 1935 or 1936 what had been only half understood, unsettling, distant stories turned horror-tragic and new assessments had to be made fast of what one believed and what one was going to do about it. The rebels of the Twenties, the generation before mine, now seemed rebels only in the Scott Fitzgerald sense: they had wasted their blood, blind to the future they could have smelled if the odor of booze hadn't been so strong. Scott knew this about himself, and understandably resented those old friends who had turned into the new radicals. But the 1920's rebels had always seemed strange to me: without charity I thought most of them were no more than a classy lot of brilliant comics, performing at low fees for the society rich. The new radicalism was what I had always been looking for.

In 1934, Hammett and I rented a charming house on Long Island and were throwing around the money from *The Thin Man*. It had been a year of heavy drinking for both of us: I drank almost as much as Hammett and our constant guests, but I was younger than most of them and didn't like myself when I drank. In any case, work on *The Children's Hour* was going bad and Hammett, who had a pleasant nature, had resolved on a new, lighter drinking program: nothing but sherry, port and beer. He was never drunker, never ate less, and was in a teasing, irritable mood. I wanted to get away from all of it. Hammett gave me the money to go to Europe.

Because I planned to stay away for a long time to

finish the play, the money had to last as long as possible. I went directly to Paris, to the small and inexpensive Hotel Jacob, and decided to see nobody. Once a day I went for a walk, twice a day I ate in working-class restaurants, struggling through French newspapers or magazines. They didn't teach me much but I did know about the formation of the Popular Front. There had been, there were to be, Fascist riots in Paris that year. Like most Americans, now and then, political troubles in Europe seemed far away from my life and certainly far away from a play about a little girl who ruined the lives of two women in a New England private school.

But after a month of nobody, I was lonely and tired of work. I telephoned Julia — we had talked several times my first weeks in Paris — to say I'd like to come to Vienna for a few days. She said that wasn't a good idea at the minute, nor a good idea to talk on a telephone that was tapped, but she'd meet me and would send a message saying where and when. I think that was the first time I ever knew a telephone could be listened in on, a life could and would be spied on. I was impressed and amused.

I waited but no word came from Julia. Then, two weeks after my phone call, the newspaper headlines said that Austrian government troops, aided by local Nazis, had bombarded the Karl Marx Hof in the Floridsdorf district of Vienna. Socialist workers, who owned the district, had defended it, and two hundred of them had been killed. I read the news in a little restaurant called the Fourth Republic, and in the middle of my dinner ran back to the hotel for my address book. But Julia's address said nothing about the Karl Marx Hof or the Floridsdorf and so I went to bed telling myself not to imagine things. At five o'clock in the morning I had a telephone call from a man who said his name was Von Zimmer, he was calling from Vienna, Julia was in a hospital.

I have no memory of the trip to Vienna, no memory of a city I was never to see again, no memory of the name of the hospital, nor how I got to it or in what language. But I remember everything after that. It was a small hospital in a mean section of town. There were about forty people in the ward. Julia's bed was the first behind the door. The right side of her face was entirely in bandages, carried around the head and on to most of the left side, leaving only the left eye and the mouth exposed. Her right arm was lying outside the bed cover, her right leg was lying on an unseen platform. There were two or three people in uniform in the room, but most of the aides were in street clothes and it was a young boy, twelve or thirteen, who brought me a stool and said to Julia, in German, "Your friend has come," as he turned her head so that she could see me with her left eye. Neither the eye nor the hand moved as she looked at me and neither of us spoke. I have no loss of memory about that first visit: there was nothing to remember. After a while, she raised her right arm toward the center of the room and I saw the boy, who was carrying a pail,

speak to a nurse. The nurse came to the bed and
moved Julia's head away from me and told me she
thought I should come back the next day. As I went
past the desk, the young boy met me in the hall and
told me to ask for a room at the Hotel Sacher. There
was another note at the desk of the hotel, a place so
much too expensive for me that I was about to take
my bags and find another. The note said that the reser-
vation had been made at the Sacher because I would
be safe there, and that was best for Julia. It was
signed John Von Zimmer.

I went back to the hospital later that evening and,
as I got off the trolley car, I saw what I had not seen
in the morning. The district was heavily ringed with
police, and men in some other uniform. The hospital
said I couldn't go into the ward, the patient was asleep
after the operation. When I asked what operation,
they asked how was I related to the patient, but my
German, and much else, had given out. I tried to find
out if the hospital desk knew John Von Zimmer's address, but they said they had never heard of him.

I was refused at the hospital the next day and the
next. Three days later a handsome, pregnant lady, in
a poor coat too small for her, took me into the ward.
The same young boy brought me the same stool, and
gently turned Julia's head toward me. Her right leg
was no longer on a platform and that made me think
everything was better. This time, after a few minutes,
she raised her right arm and touched my hand. I
stared at her hand: it had always been too large even

for this tall girl, too blunt, too heavy, ugly. She took the hand away, as if she knew what I thought, and I reached back for it. We sat for a while that way and then she pointed to her mouth, meaning that she couldn't speak because of the bandages. Then she raised her hand to the window, pointed out, and made a pushing movement with her hand.

I said, "I don't know what you mean," and realized they were the first words I had spoken to her in years. She made the motion again and then shut her eye as if she couldn't go on. After a while I fell asleep on the stool with my head against the wall. Toward afternoon a nurse came and said I had to leave. Julia's bed had been wheeled out and I think the nurse was telling me that she was being "treated."

For the three days and nights I had been in Vienna I had gone nowhere, not even for a walk, only once a day to a cheap restaurant a block from the hospital where the old man who ran it talked in English and said he had once lived in Pittsburgh. I don't believe I understood where I was, or what had happened in this city, or why, and that I was too frightened of what I didn't understand to be anything more than quiet. (Fear has always made me unable to talk or to move much, almost drowsy.) I thought constantly about how to find the man called Von Zimmer, but it seemed to me each day that he would certainly come to me. On the fourth night, about ten o'clock, I had nothing more to read, was too restless and nervous for bed, and so I took the long walk back to the restaurant near the hospital. When I got there it was closed and so I walked again until it was long past midnight, thinking how little I knew about Julia's life, how seldom we had met in the last years, how little I knew of what was happening to her now.

When I got back to the hotel the young boy from the hospital ward was standing across the street. I saw him immediately and stood waiting for him. He handed me a folded slip of paper. Then he bowed and moved away.

In the lobby of the hotel, the note, written in a weak, thin handwriting, said, "Something else is needed. They will take me tomorrow to another place. Go back to Paris *fast* and leave your address at the Sacher. Love, Julia."

I was back in Paris before I remembered that when we were kids, doing our Latin together, we would take turns translating and then correcting. Often one of us would say to the other, "Something else is needed"; we said it so often that it got to be a family joke.

I waited in Paris for a month, but no word ever came. A German friend made a telephone call for me to the hospital in Vienna, but they said they didn't know Julia's name, had no record of her ever having been there. My German friend telephoned the university twice to ask for John Von Zimmer, but once somebody said he no longer was enrolled and once they had no information about his address.

And so I went back to New York, finished *The*

Children's Hour, and three nights after it was a success I telephoned Julia's grandmother. I think the old lady was drunk — she often had been when we were young — because it took a long time to explain who I was, and then she said what difference did it make who I was, she didn't know anything about Julia, neither did the Morgan Bank, who had been transmitting huge sums of money to her all over Europe, and she thought Julia was plain crazy.

About a year later I had a letter from Julia, but it is lost now and while I am sure of what it said, I am not sure how it was said by a woman who wrote what had become almost foreign English and was telling me something she evidently thought I already knew. The letter had to do with Nazism and Germany, the necessity of a Socialist revolution throughout the world, that she had had a baby, and the baby seemed to like being called Lilly, but then she was a baby who liked almost everything. She said she had no address, but I should send letters to Paris, to 16 Rue de l'Université, in care of apartment 3. I wrote immediately to thank her about Lilly, then two more times, and finally had a postcard from her with a Zurich stamp.

I can no longer remember how long after that Anne-Marie telephoned to ask me for dinner. I think I was about to say yes when Anne-Marie told me that a friend of hers had seen Julia, that Julia was doing something called anti-Fascist work, very dangerous, and throwing away her money, did I know about the baby and wasn't that nutty, a poor unwanted illegitimate child? I said I was leaving town and couldn't have dinner. Anne-Marie said that was too bad because they didn't often visit New York, but happened to be here on the opening night of *Days to Come* and had to say, frankly, that *they* hadn't liked my play. I said that wasn't illegal, not many people had liked it, and then there was more talk about Julia, something about her leg that I didn't understand, and Anne-Marie said that she wanted me to meet her husband, who, as I certainly knew, had been a colleague of Julia's in medical school in Vienna and was now a surgeon, very successful, in San Francisco. She said he was brilliant and a real beauty. I have never liked women who talk about how men look — "so attractive" was a constant phrase of my time — and to hide my irritation I said I knew she had married but I didn't know his name. She said his name was John Von Zimmer. I am sure she heard me take a deep breath because she laughed and said the next time they came to New York she would call me, and why didn't I ever see Sammy, her brother, who was always trying to commit suicide. I was never to see Sammy again, but certainly he never committed suicide because I read about him in Suzy's society column a few months ago.

In all the years that followed I only once again saw Anne-Marie, with John Von Zimmer, in 1970, when I was teaching in Berkeley. They were in a San Francisco restaurant with six or seven other stylish-looking people, and Anne-Marie kissed me and bubbled and we exchanged addresses. Von Zimmer was silent as he stared at a wall behind my head. Neither Anne-Marie nor I did the telephoning that we said we would do the next day, but I did want very much to see Von Zimmer: I had an old question to ask, and so a few days after the meeting in the restaurant I walked around to his office. But, standing near the great Victorian house, I changed my mind. I am glad now that I didn't ask the question that almost certainly would never have been answered.

But on that day in 1937, on the train moving toward the German border, I sat looking at the hatbox. The big girl was now reading the *Frankfurter Zeitung*, the thin girl had done nothing with the book that was lying on her lap. I suppose it was the announcement of the first lunch sitting that made me look up from the past, pick up my coat, and then put it down again.

The thin girl said, "Nice coat. Warm? Of what fur?"

"It's sealskin. Yes, it's warm."

She said, pointing to the hatbox, "Your hat is also fur?"

I started to say I didn't know, realized how paralyzed I had been, know it couldn't continue, and opened the box. I took out a high, fluffy, hat of gray fox as both ladies murmured their admiration. I sat staring at it until the heavy girl said, "Put on. Nice with coat."

I suppose part of my worry, although I hadn't even

got there yet, was what to do with the knitted cap I
was wearing. I took it off and rose to fix the fur hat
in the long mirror between the windows. The top and
sides of the hat were heavy and when I put my hand
inside I felt a deep seam in the lining with heavy wads
below and around the seam. It was uncomfortable and
so I started to take it off when I remembered that the
note said I should wear the hat.

Somewhere during my hesitations the heavy girl
said she was going to lunch, could she bring me a
sandwich? I said I'd rather go to lunch but I didn't
know when we crossed the border, and immediately
realized I had made a silly and possibly dangerous
remark. The thin girl said we wouldn't be crossing
until late afternoon — she had unpacked a small box
and was eating a piece of meat — and if I was worried about my baggage she was staying in the compartment because she couldn't afford the prices in
the dining car. The heavy girl said she couldn't afford
them either, but the doctor had said she must have
hot meals and a glass of wine with her medicine. So I
went off with her to the dining car, leaving my coat
thrown over the candy box. We sat at a table with two
other people and she told me that she had been studying in Paris, had "contracted" a lung ailment, and
was going home to Cologne. She said she didn't know
what would happen to her Ph.D. dissertation because
the lung ailment had affected her bones. She talked
in a disjointed stream of words for the benefit, I
thought, of the two men who sat next to us, but even

when they left, the chatter went on as her head turned to watch everybody in a nervous tic between sentences. I was glad to be finished with lunch, so worried was I about the candy box, but it was there, untouched, when we got back to our compartment. The thin girl was asleep, but she woke up as we came in and said something in German to the heavy girl about a crowded train, and called her Louisa. It was the first indication I had that they knew each other, and I sat silent for a long time wondering why that made me uneasy. Then I told myself that if everything went on making me nervous, I'd be in a bad fix by the time it came to be nervous.

For the next few hours, the three of us dozed or read until the thin girl tapped me on the knee and said we would be crossing the border in five or ten minutes. I suppose everybody comes to fear in a different way, but I have always grown very hot or very cold, and neither has anything to do with the weather. Now, waiting, I was very hot. As the train pulled to a standstill, I got up to go outside — people were already leaving the train to pass through a check gate, and men were coming on the train to inspect baggage in the cars ahead of us — without my coat or my new hat. I was almost out the compartment door when the thin girl said, "You will need your coat and hat. It is of a windiness."

"Thank you. But I'm not cold."

Her voice changed sharply, "You will have need of your coat. Your hat is nice on your head."

I didn't ask questions because the tone in which she spoke was the answer. I turned back, put the coat around my shoulders, put on the hat that felt even heavier now with the wads of something that filled the lining, and let both girls go past me as I adjusted it in the mirror. Coming out on the platform, they were ahead of me, separated from me by several people who had come from other compartments. The heavy girl moved on. The thin girl dropped her purse and, as she picked it up, stepped to one side and moved directly behind me. We said nothing as we waited in line to reach the two uniformed men at the check gate. As the man in front of me was having his passport examined, the thin girl said, "If you have a temporary travel-through visa, it might take many minutes more than others. But that is nothing. Do not worry."

It didn't take many minutes more than others. I went through as fast as anybody else, turned in a neat line with the other travelers, went back to the train. The thin girl was directly behind me, but as we got to the steps of the train, she said, "Please," and pushed me aside to climb in first. When we reached our compartment, the fat girl was in her seat listening to two customs men in the compartment next to ours as they had some kind of good-natured discussion with a man who was opening his luggage.

The thin girl said, "They are taking great time with the luggage." As she spoke, she leaned over and picked up my candy box. She took off the ribbon and

134

said, "Thank you. I am hungry for a chocolate. Most kind."

I said, "Please, please," and knew I was never meant for this kind of thing. "I am carrying it to a friend for a gift. Please do not open it." As the customs men came into our compartment, the thin girl was chewing on a candy, the box open on her lap. I did not know much about the next few minutes except that all baggage was dragged down from the racks, that my baggage took longer than the baggage of my companions. I remember the heavy girl chatting away, and something being said about my traveling visa, and how I was going to a theatre festival because I was a playwright. (It was two days later before I realized I had never mentioned the Moscow theatre festival or anything about myself.) And the name Hellman came into the conversation I could only half understand. One of the customs men said, "Jew," and the heavy girl said certainly the name was not always of a Jew and gave examples of people and places I couldn't follow. Then the men thanked us, replaced everything neatly, and bowed themselves out the door.

Somewhere in the next hours I stopped being hot or cold and was not to be frightened again that day. The thin girl had neatly retied my candy box, but I don't think any of us spoke again until the train pulled into the station. When the porters came on for the baggage, I told myself that now I should be nervous, that if the money had been discovered at the border gate nothing much could have happened because I was still close to France. Now was the time, therefore, for caution, intelligence, reasonable fears. But it wasn't the time, and I laughed at that side of me that so often panics at a moment of no consequence, so often grows listless and sleepy near danger.

But there was to be no danger that day. The thin girl was right behind me on the long walk toward the station gate, people kissing and shaking hands all along the way. A man and a woman of about fifty came toward me, the woman holding out her arms and saying in English, "Lillian, how good it is to see you. How naughty of you not to stay more than a few hours, but even that will give us time for a nice visit — " as the thin girl, very close to me now, said, "Give her the candy box."

I said, "I am so glad to see you again. I have brought you a small gift, gifts — " but the box was now out of my hands and I was being moved toward the gate. Long before we reached the gate the woman and the thin girl had disappeared.

The man said, "Go through the gate. Ask the man at the gate if there is a restaurant near the station. If he says Albert's go to it. If he gives you another name, go to that one, look at it, and turn back to Albert's, which is directly opposite the door you are facing." As I asked the official at the gate about a restaurant, the man went past me. The official said please to step to one side, he was busy, would take care of me in a minute. I didn't like being in the station so I crossed the street to Albert's. I went through a revolving door and was so shocked at the sight of Julia at a table that I stopped at the door. She half rose, called softly, and I went toward her with tears that I couldn't stop because I saw two crutches lying next to her and now knew what I had never wanted to know before. Half out of her seat, holding to the table, she said, "Fine, fine. I have ordered caviar for us to celebrate, Albert had to send for it, it won't be long."

She held my hand for several minutes, and said, "Fine. Everything has gone fine. Nothing will happen now. Let's eat and drink and see each other. So many years."

I said, "How long have we got? How far is the other station, the one where I get the train to Moscow?"

"You have two hours, but we haven't that long together because you have to be followed to the station and the ones who follow you must have time to find the man who will be with you on the train until Warsaw in the morning."

I said, "You look like nobody else. You are more beautiful now."

She said, "Stop crying about my leg. It was amputated and the false leg is clumsily made so I am coming to New York in the next few months, as soon as I can, and get a good one. Lilly, don't cry for me. *Stop the tears.* We must finish the work now. Take off the hat the way you would if it was too hot for this place. Comb your hair, and put the hat on the seat between us."

Her coat was open, and the minute I put the hat on the bench she pinned it deep inside her coat with a safety pin that was ready for it.

She said, "Now I am going to the toilet. If the waiter tries to help me up, wave him aside and come with me. The toilet locks. If anybody should try to open it, knock on the door and call to me, but I don't think that will happen."

She got up, picked up one of the crutches, and waved me to the other arm. She spoke in German to a man I guess was Albert as we moved down the long room. She pulled the crutch too quickly into the toilet door, it caught at a wrong angle, and she made a gesture with the crutch, tearing at it in irritation.

When she came out of the toilet, she smiled at me. As we walked back to the table, she spoke in a loud voice, saying something in German about the toilet and then, in English, "I forget you don't know German. I was saying that German public toilets are always clean, much cleaner than ours, particularly under the new regime. The bastards, the murderers."

Caviar and wine were on the table when we sat down again and she was cheerful with the waiter. When he had gone away she said, "Ah, Lilly. Fine, fine. Nothing will happen now. But it is your right to know that it is my money you brought in and we can save five hundred, and maybe, if we can bargain right, a thousand people with it. So believe that you have been better than a good friend to me, you have done something important."

"Jews?"

"About half. And political people. Socialists, Communists, plain old Catholic dissenters. Jews aren't the only people who have suffered here." She sighed. "That's enough of that. We can only do today what we can do today and today you did it for us. Do you need something stronger than wine?"

I said I didn't and she said to talk fast now, there wasn't much time, to tell her as much as possible. I told her about my divorce, about the years with Hammett. She said she had read *The Children's Hour,* she was pleased with me, and what was I going to do next?

I said, "I did it. A second play, a failure. Tell me about your baby."

"She's fat and handsome. I've got over minding that she looks like my mother."

"I want very much to see her."

"You will," she said, "I'll bring her when I come home for the new leg and she can live with you, if you like."

I said, meaning no harm, "Couldn't I see her now?"

"Are you crazy? Do you think I would bring her here? Isn't it enough I took chances with your safety? I will pay for that tonight and tomorrow and . . ." Then she smiled. "The baby lives in Mulhouse, with some nice folks. I see her that way whenever I cross the border. Maybe, when I come back for the leg, I'll leave her with you. She shouldn't be in Europe. It ain't for babies now."

"I haven't a house or even an apartment of any permanence," I said, "but I'll get one if you bring the baby."

"Sure. But it wouldn't matter. You'd be good to her." Then she laughed. "Are you as angry a woman as you were a child?"

"I think so," I said. "I try not to be, but there it is."

"Why do you try not to be?"

"If you lived around me, you wouldn't ask."

"I've always liked your anger," she said, "trusted it."

"You're the only one, then, who has."

"Don't let people talk you out of it. It may be uncomfortable for them, but it's valuable to you. It's what made you bring the money in today. Yes, I'll leave the baby with you. Its father won't disturb you, he wants nothing to do with the baby or with me. He's O.K. Just an ordinary climber. I don't know why I did it, Freud told me not to, but I don't care. The baby's good."

She smiled and patted my hand. "Someday I will take you to meet Freud. What am I saying? I will probably never see him again — I have only so much longer to last in Europe. The crutches make me too noticeable. The man who will take care of you has just come into the street. Do you see him outside the window? Get up and go now. Walk across the street, get a taxi, take it to Bahnhof 200. Another man will be waiting there. He will make sure you get safely on the train and will stay with you until Warsaw tomorrow morning. He is in car A, compartment 13. Let me see your ticket."

I gave it to her. "I think that will be in the car to your left." She laughed. *"Left,* Lilly, *left.* Have you ever learned to tell left from right, south from north?"

"No. I don't want to leave you. The train doesn't go for over an hour. I want to stay with you a few more minutes."

"No," she said. "Something could still go wrong and we must have time to get help if that should happen. I'll be coming to New York in a few months. Write from Moscow to American Express in Paris. I have stuff picked up every few weeks." She took my hand and raised it to her lips. "My beloved friend."

Then she pushed me and I was on my feet. When I got to the door I turned and must have taken a step back because she shook her head and moved her face to look at another part of the room.

I did not see the man who followed me to the station. I did not see the other man on the train, although several times a youngish man passed my compartment and the same man took the vacant chair next to me at dinner, but didn't speak to me at all.

When I went back to my compartment from dinner the conductor asked if I wanted my two small valises put in the corridor for examination when we crossed the German-Polish border so that I wouldn't be awakened. I told him I had a wardrobe trunk in the baggage car, handed him the key for the customs people, and went to sleep on the first sleeping pill of my life, which may be why I didn't wake up until just before we pulled into the Warsaw station at seven in the morning. There was bustle in the station as I raised the curtain to look out. Standing below my window was the young man who had sat next to me at dinner. He made a gesture with his hand, but I didn't understand and shook my head. Then he looked around and pointed to his right. I shook my head again, bewildered, and he moved away from the window. In a minute there was a knock on my door and I rose to open it. An English accent said through the crack, "Good morning. Wanted to say goodbye to you, have a happy trip." And then, very, very softly, "Your trunk was removed by the Germans. You are in no danger because you are across the border. Do nothing for a few hours and then ask the Polish conductor about the trunk. Don't return from Moscow through Germany, travel another way." In a loud voice he said, "My best regards to your family," and disappeared.

For two hours I sat in bed, doubtful, frightened of the next move, worried about the loss of clothes in my trunk. When I got dressed, I asked the Polish conductor if the German conductor had left my trunk key with him. He was upset when he told me the German customs people had removed the trunk, that often happened, but he was sure it would be sent on to me in

Moscow after a few days, nothing unusual, the German swine often did it now.

The trunk did arrive in Moscow two weeks later. The lining was in shreds, the drawers were broken, but only a camera was missing and four or five books. I did not know then, and I do not know now, whether the trunk had anything to do with Julia because I was not to see Germany for thirty years and I was never to speak with Julia again.

I wrote to her from Moscow, again from Prague on my way back to Paris, and after I had returned to New York from Spain during the Civil War. Three or four months later I had a card with a Geneva postmark. It said, says, "Good girl to go to Spain. Did it convince you? We'll talk about that when I return to New York in March."

But March and April came and went and there was no word from Julia. I telephoned her grandmother, but I should have known better. The old lady said they hadn't heard from Julia in two years and why did I keep worrying her? I said I had seen Julia in October and she hung up the phone. Somewhere about that time I saw a magazine picture of Julia's mother, who had just married again, an Argentine, but I saw no reason for remembering his name.

On May 23, 1938, I had a cable, dated London two days before and sent to the wrong address. It said, "Julia has been killed stop please advise Moore's funeral home Whitechapel Road London what disposition stop my sorrow for you for all of us." It was signed John Watson but had no address.

It is never possible for me to cry at the time when it could do me some good, so, instead, I got very drunk for two days and don't remember anything about them. The third morning I went around to Julia's grandmother's house and was told by the butler, who came out on the street as if I were a danger to the house, that the old people were on a world cruise and wouldn't be back for eight weeks. I asked the name of the boat, was asked for my credentials, and by the time we batted all that around, I was screaming that their granddaughter was dead and that he and they could go fuck themselves. I was so sick that night that Dash, who never wanted me to go anywhere because he never wanted to, said he thought I should go to London right away.

I have no diary notes of that trip and now only the memory of standing over a body with a restored face that didn't hide the knife wound that ran down the left side. The funeral man explained that he had tried to cover the face slash but I should see the wounds on the body if I wanted to see a mess that couldn't be covered. I left the place and stood on the street for a while. When I went back in the funeral man handed me a note over the lunch he was eating. The note said, "Dear Miss Hellman. We have counted on your coming but perhaps it is not possible for you, so I will send a carbon of this to your New York address. None of us knows what disposition her family wishes to make, where they want what should be a hero's funeral. It is your right to know that the Nazis found her in Frankfurt, in the apartment of a colleague. We got her to London in the hope of saving her. Sorry that I cannot be here to help you. It is better that I take my sorrow for this wonderful woman into action and perhaps revenge. Yours, John Watson, who speaks here for many others. Salud."

I went away that day and toward evening telephoned the funeral man to ask if he had an address for John Watson. He said he had never heard the name John Watson, he had picked up the body at the house of a Dr. Chester Lowe at 30 Downshire Hill. When I got there it was a house that had been made into apartments, but there was no Dr. Lowe on the name plates, and for the first time it occurred to me that my investigations could be bad for people who were themselves in danger.

So I brought the body home with me on the old *De Grasse* and tried this time to reach Julia's mother. The same butler told me that he couldn't give me her mother's address, although he knew the mother had been informed of the death. I had the body cremated and the ashes are still where they were that day so long ago.

I should, of course, have gone to Mulhouse before I came home from London, but I didn't, didn't even think about it in those awful days in London or on the boat. After the cremation, I wrote to Julia's grandmother, told her about the baby and that I knew nothing more than that she lived with a family in Mulhouse, but Mulhouse couldn't be so big that they would have trouble finding an American child. I had no answer. I guess I knew I wouldn't, and so I wrote another letter, this time nasty, and got an answer from a fancy name in a fancy law firm saying that everything would be done "in this strange case" about a child only I believed existed and I would be kept informed of any "doubtful results."

In the next few months, I found I dreamed every night about Julia, who was almost always the age when I first met her. Hammett said I looked awful and if it worried me that much why didn't I find a lawyer or a detective in Mulhouse. William Wyler, the movie director, with whom I had made two pictures, had been born in Mulhouse and his family still owned a department store there. It is too long ago for me to be accurate about when and how he got me the name of a lawyer in Mulhouse, but he did, and after a while the lawyer wrote that the investigation was proving difficult, but he thought, in the end, they would certainly find the baby if she was still there.

Three months later the war broke out and I never heard again from anybody in Western Europe until I arrived in London from Russia in March 1944. My second day there — my reason for being there was to do a documentary film for the British government about people on the docksides during the V–2 bomb-

ings — I realized I was somewhere in the neighborhood of the funeral parlor. I found it, but it had been
bombed to pieces.

Nothing is left of all this except that sometime in
the early 1950's, I was sitting on a stone wall at a
Long Island picnic at Ruth and Marshall Field's. A
man next to me was talking about a man called Onassis — the first time I had heard his name — and a
lawsuit by the U.S. government against Onassis, and
when he was finished with that he turned to me and
said, "My father was the lawyer to whom you wrote
about Julia. I am Julia's third cousin."
    After a while I said, "Yes."
    He said, "My father died last year."
    "Your father never wrote to me again."
    He said, "You see, I'm not a lawyer, I'm a banker."
    I said, "Whatever happened to her family?"
    "The grandparents are dead. Julia senior lives in
Argentina — "
    "The bastards," I said, "all of them."
    He smiled at me. "They are my cousins."
    "Did they ever find the baby they didn't want to
find? I don't care who you are."
    "I never knew anything about a baby," he said.
    I said, "I don't believe you," got off the stone fence,
left a note for Ruthie saying I didn't feel well, and
drove home.

THEATRE

IT is strange to me that so many people like to listen to so many other people talk about the theatre. There are those who talk for large fees or give it away at small dinner parties and often their stories are charming and funny, but they are seldom people who have done much solid work. You are there, you are good in the theatre, you have written or directed or acted or designed just because you have and there is little that you can or should be certain about because almost everything in the theatre contradicts something else. People have come together, as much by accident as by design, done the best they can and sometimes the worst, profited or not, gone their way vowing to see each other the next week, mean it, and wave across a room a few years later.

The manuscript, the words on the page, was what

you started with and what you have left. The production is of great importance, has given the play the only life it will know, but it is gone, in the end, and the pages are the only wall against which to throw the future or measure the past.

How the pages got there, in their form, in their order, is more of a mystery than reason would hope for. That is why I have never wanted to write about the theatre and find the teaching of English literature more rewarding than teaching drama. (Drama usually means "the theatre," the stories about it, chatter of failure and success.) You are good in boats not alone from knowledge, but because water is a part of you, you are easy on it, fear it and like it in such equal parts that you work well in a boat without thinking about it and may be even safer because you don't need to think too much. That is what we mean by instinct and there is no way to explain an instinct for the theatre, although those who have it recognize each other and a bond is formed between them. The need of theatre instinct may be why so many good writers have been such inferior playwrights — the light that a natural dramatist can see on a dark road is simply not there.

There are, of course, other reasons why I have not written about the theatre: I have known for many years that part of me struggled too hard within it, and the reasons for that I do not know and they could not, in any case, be of interest to anybody but me. I always knew that I was seldom comfortable with theatre people although I am completely comfortable in a theatre; and I am now at an age when the cutting up of old touches must be carefully watched and any sentence that begins "I remember" lasts too long for my taste, even when I myself say it.

But I have certain pictures, portraits, mementos of my plays. They are what I have left of the long years, the pleasure in the work and the pains.

The Children's Hour was my first play. I don't remember very much about the writing or the casting, but I remember Lee Shubert, who owned the theatre, as he did many other theatres in New York, coming down the aisle to stare at me during a rehearsal day. I was sitting mid-theatre with my feet on the top of the chair in front of me. He came around to stand directly before me and said, "Take your dirty shoes off my chair."

I said, "My shoes aren't touching the chair, Mr. Shubert," but, after a pause, he pushed my right leg to the floor.

I said, "I don't like strange men fooling around with my right leg so don't do it again."

Mr. Shubert called out to Herman Shumlin, who was directing the play from the front row. They met in the aisle and I heard Herman say, "That girl, as you call her, is the author of the play," and went back to directing. About half an hour later, Mr. Shubert,

who had been standing in the back watching the play
for which he had put up the money, came down and
sat behind me.

"This play," he said to the back of my head, "could
land us all in jail." He had been watching the con-
fession scene, the recognition of the love of one woman
for another.

I said, "I am eating a frankfurter and I don't want
to think about jail. Would you like a piece of it?"

"I forbid you to get mustard on my chairs," he said
and I was never to see him again until the play had
been running for about six months and then I heard
him ask the doorman who I was.

I've always told myself that I was so drunk on the
opening night of *The Children's Hour* because I had
begun to drink two nights before. I had gone to have
dinner with my mother and father, who had not read
the play, had not seen the rehearsals, had asked no
questions, but, obviously, had talked to each other
when they were alone. Both of them were proud of
me, but in my family you didn't show such things,
and both of them, I think, were frightened for me in
a world they didn't know.

In any case, my mother, who frequently made sentences that had nothing to do with what went before,
said, in space, "Well, all I know is that you were considered the sweetest-smelling baby in New Orleans."

She had, through my life, told me this several times
before, describing how two strange ladies had paused
in front of our house to stare at me in the baby car-

riage and then to lean down and sniff me. One of them had said, "That's the sweetest-smelling baby in town." The other had said, "In all New Orleans," and when my mother told our neighbor about her pleasure in this exchange, the neighbor had said of course it was true, famously true, I always smelled fresh as a flower. I didn't know that my mother had never until that night told my father or, if she had, he was less nervous than he was two nights before the opening. Now, when she repeated it, he said, *"Who* was the sweetest-smelling baby in New Orleans?"

"Lillian," said my mother.

"Lillian? Lillian?" said my father. *"I* was the sweetest-smelling baby in New Orleans and you got that information from my mother and sisters and have stolen it."

"Stolen it?" said my shocked mother. "I never stole anything in my life and you know it. Lillian was the sweetest-smelling baby in New Orleans and I can prove it."

"It's disgraceful," said my father, "what you are doing. You have taken what people said about *me, always said about me,* and given it to your own child."

"Your child, too," said my mother.

"That's no reason for lying and stealing," said my father. "I must ask you now to take it back and not to repeat it again."

My mother was a gentle woman and would do almost anything to avoid a fight, but now she was aroused as I had never before seen her.

"I will take nothing back. You are depriving your own child of her rightful honor and I think it disgraceful."

My father rose from the table. "I will telephone Jenny and prove it to you," he said.

He was giving the phone operator the number of his sisters' house in New Orleans when my mother yelled, "Jenny and Hannah will say anything you tell them to. I won't have it. Lillian was the sweetest-smelling baby in New Orleans and that's that." She began to cry.

I said, "I think maybe you're both crazy." I went to the sideboard and poured myself a large straight whiskey. My father, holding the phone, said to me, "Sweet-smelling, are you? You've been drinking too much for years."

"Don't pay him any mind, baby," said my mother, "any man who would deny his own child."

I left before my father spoke to his sisters and only found out months later that although my mother and father came to the opening night together, and both of them kissed me, they didn't speak to each other for several days.

On the afternoon of the opening night of *The Children's Hour* I drowned the hangover with brandy. I think I saw the play from the back of the theatre, holding to the rail, but I am not sure: I do remember the final curtain and an audience yelling, "Author, author." It was not all modesty that kept me from the curtain call — I couldn't have made backstage without falling. I wish I had understood and been happy in all the excited noise that comes only when the author is unknown and will never come again in quite so generous a fashion. I remember Robert Benchley pressing my arm and nodding his head as he passed me on his way out of the theatre. It was a nice thing for a critic to do, but I don't think I knew what he meant. I knew only half-things that happened that night: I went to the Plaza Hotel, but I can't remember who was at the table; I went to Tony's with some people who were at the Plaza; I went to Herman's apartment and he told me that the papers were very good indeed and we would be a big hit and he had a bad headache. For the next few hours I have no account. Then I was in a strange bar, not unusual for me in those days, and I was talking to a man and two women. Or they were talking to me and the conversation had to do with the metallic fringe that was on the bottom of the younger woman's dress. Then I was asleep, sitting up, on my couch in the Elysée Hotel. When I woke up one of the women was watering the plants on the windowsill and the other woman was crying, standing against a wall. I said to the man, "Are these your sisters?" and he laughed.

"What's funny about that?"

"Sez you," he said, "sez you."

"I'm going to marry him," said the one who was standing against the wall, "and it's already shit. Everybody has missed the boat, everywhere, everywhere, everywhere and somehow."

"Ssh," I said, "I owe this hotel a lot of money."

"The boat," she screamed, "everybody, everywhere."

There was some more of that. I went to make coffee and when I came back the pair who were going to get married were sitting on the couch holding hands and the one who had been watering the plants was reading my first-night telegrams at the desk. (I was to meet her again a few years later. She was a handsome, boyish-looking woman at every society-literary cocktail party. Her name was Emily Vanderbilt and she was to marry Raoul Whitfield, a mystery story writer. A few years after the marriage she was murdered on a ranch they bought in New Mexico, and neither the mystery story expert nor the police ever found the murderer.) Nobody spoke until the potential bride suddenly pushed her fiancé off the couch, and the one reading the telegrams screamed, "Moxie! Moxie!"

I said — I think it was the sentence I most often used in those years — "Why don't you all go home?"

The man had picked himself up from the floor, was pouring himself a drink, Moxie and her friend were arguing about something or other, when I went in the bedroom shouting, "Why don't you all go home," and locked the door. It was still dark, maybe six o'clock, when I woke up with an awful headache and cramps in my legs, remembering that I should have telephoned Hammett, who was in Hollywood, to tell him the play was a hit. I wanted a cold beer and went through the living room to get it. I thought the room was empty, but as I was returning to bed with my beer, I saw the man sitting at the desk staring out of the window.

I coughed and he turned to me, raising his empty highball glass. "Want to get me a fresh drinkie?"

"What did you do with your ladies?"

"I certainly would like an eensy drink."

"I don't feel well. I have work to do. I have to make a phone call. I had a play open last night."

"You kept saying that," he said. "I'm a doctor."

"*You're* a doctor?"

"Opening an office next week, Park and 80th, going in with my uncle, the heart specialist. Come and see me."

I said I didn't think I'd do that and put a call through to Hammett in the rented house with the soda fountain in the Pacific Palisades. After a long time a woman answered the phone and said she was Mr. Hammett's secretary, what a strange hour to be calling. I sat on the couch thinking about that and feeling very dizzy from the beer.

The doctor said, "What's your name?"

I went back to the bedroom, closed the door, and knew the question had sobered me up. I had wasted what should have been the nicest night of my life. I disliked then and dislike now those who spoil pleasure or luck when it comes not so much because they refuse it — they are a different breed — but because they cannot see it or abandon it for blind nonsense. I had done just that and wanted now to find out about it.

The doctor opened the door. "Do you want to go out for breakfast or Atlantic City? What's your name?"

I said, "What's yours?"

"Peregrine Perry. From Lord Perry of long ago."

"Do they call you Perry Perry?"

"Oh, Christ," he said, "all you have to do is wait for it."

He closed the door, and when I woke up that afternoon the apartment was empty.

(Ten years later I bought a house on 82nd Street and somewhere in that first year I saw him come out of an office with a sign on it that said "Dr. P. John Perry" and get into a car driven by a chauffeur.)

But long before that, two days after the woman had told me she was Hammett's secretary, I realized that I had called Hammett at three A.M. California time and that he had no secretary. We had spoken on the phone a number of times in those days — he was very happy about *The Children's Hour*, proud that all his trouble with me had paid off — but on the day I understood about the secretary and three o'clock in the morning I took a plane to Los Angeles. By the time I got to the house in the Pacific Palisades it was night and I had had a good deal to drink. I went immediately to the soda fountain — Hammett had rented the house from Harold Lloyd — smashed it to pieces and flew back to New York on a late night plane.

The failure of a second work is, I think, more damaging to a writer than failure ever will be again. It is then that the success of the first work seems an accident and, if the fears you had as you wrote it were dissipated by the praise, now you remember that the praise did not always come from the best minds and even when it did it could have been that they were not telling the truth or that you had played good tricks. And you are probably too young, too young at writing, to have found out that you really only care what a few people think; only they, with the change in names that time brings about, will stand behind your chair for good or bad, forever. But failure in the theatre is more public, more brilliant, more unreal than in any other field. The praise is usually out of bounds: the photographs, interviews, "appearances," party invitations are so swift and dazzling that you go into the second work with confidence you will never have again if you have any sense.

Days to Come was written in Princeton, New Jersey. Hammett, who never wanted much to live in New York, had rented the lovely house of a rich professor who was a Napoleon expert. Its overformal Directoire furniture was filled each night with students who liked Hammett, but liked even better the free alcohol and the odd corners where they could sleep and bring their friends. That makes it sound like now, when students are often interesting, but it wasn't: they were a dull generation, but Dash never much examined the people to whom he was talking if he was drunk enough to talk at all.

Even now the pains I had on the opening night of

Days to Come puzzle me. Good theatre jokes are almost always based on survived disasters, and there
were so many that night that they should, in time,
have passed into comedy: the carefully rehearsed light
cues worked as if they were meant for another play;
the props, not too complicated, showed up where nobody had ever seen them before and broke, or didn't
break, with the malice of animated beings; good actors
knew by the first twenty minutes they had lost the audience and thus became bad actors; the audience, maybe
friendly as it came in, was soon restless and uncomfortable. The air of a theatre is unmistakable: things
go well or they do not. They did not. Standing in the
back of the side aisle, I vomited without knowing it
was going to happen and went home to change my
clothes. I wanted, of course, to go to bed and stay
there, but I was young enough to worry about cow-
ardice and so I got back in time to see William Ran-
dolph Hearst lead his six guests out of the theatre,
in the middle of the second act, talking very loud as
they came up the aisle.

It is hard for me to believe these many years later
in the guilt I felt for the failure of *Days to Come;*
the threads of those threads have lasted to this day.
Guilt is often an excuse for not thinking and maybe
that's what happened to me. In any case, it was to be
two years before I could write another play, *The Little
Foxes,* and when I did get to it I was so scared that
I wrote it nine times.

Up to a year ago I used to think of *Days to Come*

as the play that taught me not to vomit. (I have never vomited again.) Reading it then, for a book that includes all my plays, I liked it: it is crowded and overwrought, but it is a good report of rich liberals in the 1930's, of a labor leader who saw through them, of a modern lost lady, and has in it a correct prediction of how conservative the American labor movement was to become.

Soon after *The Children's Hour* I had had an offer to write movies for Samuel Goldwyn. I think Mr. Goldwyn was in his early fifties when we first met, but he was so vigorous and springy that I was not conscious of his age for many years. He was, as were many of the bright, rough, tough lot that first saw the potential of the motion picture camera, a man of great power. Often the power would rise to an inexplicable pitch of panic anger when he was crossed or disappointed, and could then decline within minutes to the whispered, pained moral talk of a loony clergyman whimpering that God had betrayed him. What I liked best were not Mr. Goldwyn's changes of English speech, although some of them were mighty nice and often better than the original. Certainly "I took it all with a dose of salts" is just as good as a grain; the more famous "a verbal contract isn't worth the paper it is written on" makes sense; he meant to be courteous the day he called down "Bon voyage to all of you" to those of us on the dock, as he, a passenger, sailed away; and when, soon after the war, he was asked to make a toast to Field Marshal Montgomery, and rose, lifted his glass, and said, "A long life to Marshall Field Montgomery Ward," one knew exactly why. But I liked best his calculated eccentricities. When he needed a favor or had to make a difficult bargain and knew a first move was not the best position from which to deal, he was brilliant. I was in his office when he wanted an actor under contract to Darryl Zanuck and demanded that Zanuck's secretary call him out of a meeting. After a long wait, Mr. Goldwyn said into the phone, "Yes, Darryl? What can I do for you today?" And a few years after the McCarthy period, during which I was banned in Hollywood, my phone rang in Martha's Vineyard. Mr. Goldwyn's secretary and I had a pleasant reunion, she said he had been trying to reach me for two days to ask if I wanted to write *Porgy and Bess.* After a long wait Mr. Goldwyn's voice said, "Hello, Lillian, hello. Nice of you to call me after all these years. How can I help you?"

But I think our early days together worked well because I was a difficult young woman who didn't care as much about money as the people around me and so, by accident, I took a right step within the first months of working for Mr. Goldwyn. I had been hired to rewrite an old silly, hoping I could make it O.K., to be directed by Sidney Franklin, a famous man who had done many of the Norma Shearer pictures. It was then, and often still is, the custom to talk for weeks and months before the writer is allowed to touch the typewriter. Such conferences were called breaking the

164

back of the story and that is, indeed, an accurate description. We, a nice English playwright called Mordaunt Shairp and I, would arrive at Franklin's house each morning at ten, have a refined health lunch a few hours later, and leave at five. The next day whatever we had decided would sometimes be altered and sometimes be scrapped because Franklin had consulted a friend the night before or discussed our decisions with his bridge partners. After six or seven weeks of this, Franklin said it was rude of me to lie all day on his couch with my back turned to him, napping. I left his house saying I was sorry, it was rude, but I couldn't go on that way. I took the night plane to New York, locked myself in with some books, and the first telephone call I answered two days later was from Mr. Goldwyn, who said if I came back immediately I could go to a room by myself, start writing, and he'd give me a raise. I said I'd think about it, didn't, and left for Paris. When he found me there a week later he offered a long-term contract with fine clauses about doing nothing but stories I liked and doing them where and when I liked. I had become valuable to Mr. Goldwyn because I had left him for reasons he didn't understand. For many years that made me an unattainable woman, as desirable as such women are, in another context, for men who like them that way.

They were good years and most of the time I enjoyed Mr. Goldwyn. The extraordinary conflicts in a man who wished to make "fine pictures" and climb into an educated or social world while grappling at the same time with a nature made rough by early poverty and tough by later big money amused me, and made him far more interesting than more "civilized" men like Irving Thalberg. (I never understood Scott Fitzgerald's *The Last Tycoon* version of Thalberg: the romanticism that went into that portrait had, in my mind, little to do with the obvious man who had once offered me a job by telling me how lucky I would be to work with him.) But, as in the theatre, I have few memories of the actual work I did in pictures, although I have sharp recollections of much that happened outside the work. And maybe, in the end, they are the same tale.

I had known George Haight in New York as a bright young man from Yale who had written *Goodbye Again,* a funny play. One of his friends, his ex-college roommate, I think, was a director, Henry C. Potter, and now all three of us were in Hollywood, George working as some kind of executive for Goldwyn. No two men, Haight and Potter, could have been more unalike: George was loose-limbed, sloppy, gay, wonderful at magicians' tricks, full of nice jokes; Potter was prep-school handsome, respectable, grandson of a bishop, an unexpected man for the world of the theatre or Hollywood. I was glad to find George working for Goldwyn: it was nice to wander into his office for an hour's exhibition of his newest card tricks or to have him wander into mine for a long afternoon's sleep.

I no longer remember what year I went to Cuba for

a vacation after the opening of what play and on my way to write what movie script. It was the custom then in some parts of Europe and most of Latin America to sell small boxes of wax matches with pictures of movie stars pasted to the box. I don't know what publicity department sent Henry C. Potter's picture out to what match factory — he did look like the cleanest of juveniles — but I came across two boxes and, to please George Haight, gave the head bellboy at the Hotel Nacional five dollars and the promise of a dollar a box for any more he could find. I arrived in Hollywood with nine Henry C. Potter matchboxes and for days George had them laid out on his desk brooding over them. Then he told me that Potter was giving a cocktail party in a few weeks and he thought he had the answer: we were to stamp twenty-seven condoms with the words "Compliments of Henry C. Potter," roll them three to a box, and he, Haight, would distribute them on tables at the cocktail party. Since George was very skillful with his hands and knew where all gadgets were to be bought, we did not foresee, that day of our pleasure, the awful work that was to come.

George bought the stamps, the delicate knives, a small stove to melt the wax that would be used to make the words and, during the first few days, the condoms in the drugstore opposite the studio. I was not skillful, but to my surprise he wasn't either. The carefully carved stamps broke the condoms because hot wax made holes and cool wax wouldn't take. After a time our drugstore ran out of condoms and one of the lasting minutes my eyes will hold is the picture of the owner as he stared at George on his last request for twelve boxes.

When George was unable to persuade me that it was my turn to find a new place to buy condoms, we had a cool day of not talking to each other. But the following morning he showed up with a dozen more boxes, fresh stamps, a more delicate knife, and a new theory for the process. By the third or fourth day of our second week we had given up all other work. Haight's secretary had, from the first, been posted at the door to keep out visitors, but now I refused two conferences with Mr. Goldwyn on the grounds that I first had to try out my ideas on Haight, who had nothing to do with the picture I was writing. And by that time we were not in a good humor with each other — I thought he was not as skillful as he once was, and he said I was clumsy and that he should have known it. One day, in fact, miserable and tired, we raised our voices to the point where the music department, situated in the building directly behind, came to their windows to watch the waving about of ruined condoms, and I yelled at them to mind their business.

I can no longer remember how we solved the stamping, but we did, and there were twenty-seven perfect condoms laid out on a table, all reading in green "Compliments of Henry C. Potter." We quit work early that day, but after enough celebrating drinks we forgot why we had left the studio and went to gamble in the Clover Club and got back to the studio about five in the morning because George said we only had two more days before the cocktail party and I had wasted enough of Mr. Goldwyn's money. It was good we went back so early because a new and even more trying period was ahead: how to roll the things so that three, even two, could go neatly in the small boxes. We rolled them around toothpicks, we whittled sticks, we shaved down pencils, we straightened paper clips and hairpins, but it was obvious they were too wide for the matchboxes.

They were bad days, growing dangerous: Goldwyn's legal department wanted to see me about something or other and reported to Goldwyn that I said I was home with an abscessed tooth. That didn't fit with Goldwyn's having seen me arrive at the studio on William Wyler's motorcycle, so when he called to ask me why I didn't go immediately to a dentist, I forgot what I had told the legal department and said I didn't understand how a dentist could cure a badly sprained neck. Sam said that was odd, would I come immediately and talk to him, something strange was going on. George said I was a dope of a liar; I said I was not meant to spend my life on condoms and was ready to throw over the whole thing. He said I was a fink, and while we were being nasty to each other my elderly secretary, who knew nothing more through those days than that I was missing from my office, opened George's door to say *his* secretary wasn't feeling well and couldn't come to work, and stared down at the condoms. She was an unfriendly woman, but I heard George say to her,

"We have a problem. Have you ever rolled a condom?" I left his office to hide in the toilet and came back to find that she had solved the problem: we were not to roll the condoms, we were to fold them lengthwise, crosswise, and stack them.

George took them to the cocktail party, but either Potter never knew about the condoms or was smart enough not to give George the pleasure of his complaint. In any case, George and I never spoke about them again.

Ten of the twelve plays I have written are connected to Hammett — he was in the Army in the Aleutian Islands during the Second World War for one of them, and he was dead when I wrote the last — but *The Little Foxes* was the one that was most dependent on him. We were living together in the same house, he was not doing any work of his own, but after his death, when much became clear to me that had not been before, I knew that he was working so hard for me because *Days to Come* had scared me and scared him for my future.

If that is true — there is a chance I have made the dependency greater than it was — then it is the more remarkable because it was a strange time of our years together. I don't know if I was paying him back for his casual ladies of our early years — it takes a jealous nature a long time to understand that there can be casual ladies — but certainly I was serious or semiserious about another man and Hammett knew it. Neither of us ever talked about it until I told Dash that I had decided not to marry the man.

He looked at me in surprise. "*Marry? You* decided? There was never a chance you'd marry him."

"It was about to happen," I said. "We had set the day and the place. I thought you knew that."

"I would never have allowed that. Never."

I laughed and he knew why I laughed because a few days later he said, "It was no good. It would never have been any good. The day it is good for you, I'll allow it."

"Thank you," I said, "but if that happens I won't ask your permission and therefore won't thank you for giving it."

"Without my permission you won't ever do it. And you ought to know that by now."

For years after I would say such things as, "May I have your permission this morning to go to the hairdresser, then to the library and on my way home buy an ice cream cone?" But he was not a vain man and, as time moved on, I knew he had been right.

The Little Foxes was the most difficult play I ever wrote. I was clumsy in the first drafts, putting in and taking out characters, ornamenting, decorating, growing more and more weary as the versions of scenes and then acts and then three whole plays had to be thrown away.

Some of the trouble came because the play has a distant connection to my mother's family and every-

171

thing that I had heard or seen or imagined had formed a giant tangled time-jungle in which I could find no space to walk without tripping over old roots, hearing old voices speak about histories made long before my day.

In the first three versions of the play, because it had been true in life, Horace Giddens had syphilis. When Regina, his wife, who had long refused him her bed, found out about it she put fresh paint on a miserable building that had once been used as slave quarters and kept him there for the rest of his life because, she said, he might infect his children. I had been told that the real Regina would speak with outrage of her betrayal by a man she had never liked and then would burst out laughing at what she said. On the day he died, she dropped the moral complaints forever and went horseback riding during his funeral. All that seemed fine for the play. But it wasn't: life had been too big, too muddled for writing. So the syphilis became heart trouble. I cut out the slave cabin and the long explanations of Regina and Horace's early life together.

I was on the eighth version of the play before Hammett gave a nod of approval and said he thought maybe everything would be O.K. if only I'd cut out the "blackamoor chitchat." Even then I knew that the toughness of his criticism, the coldness of his praise, gave him a certain pleasure. But even then I, who am not a good-tempered woman, admired his refusal with me, or with anybody else, to decorate or apologize or placate. It came from the most carefully guarded honesty I have ever known, as if one lie would muck up his world. If the honesty was mixed with harshness, I didn't much care, it didn't seem to me my business. The desire to take an occasional swipe is there in most of us, but most of us have no reason for it, it is as aimless as the pleasure of a piece of candy. When it is controlled by sense and balance, it is still not pretty, but it is not dangerous and often it is useful. It was useful to me and I knew it.

The casting of the play was difficult: we offered it to Ina Claire and to Judith Anderson. Each had a pleasant reason for refusing: each meant that the part was unsympathetic, a popular fear for actresses before that concept became outmoded. Herman Shumlin asked me what I thought of Tallulah Bankhead, but I had never seen her here or in her famous English days. She had returned to New York by 1939, had done a couple of flops, and was married to a nice, silly-handsome actor called John Emery. She was living in the same hotel I was, but I had fallen asleep by the time Herman rang my bell after six hours spent upstairs with Tallulah on their first meeting. He said he had a headache, was worn out by Miss Bankhead's vitality, but he thought she would do fine for us if he could, in the future, avoid the kind of scene he had just come from: she had been "wild" about the play, wild enough to insist the consultation take place while she was in bed with John Emery and a bottle. Shumlin said he didn't think Emery liked that much, but he was certain that poor Emery was unprepared for Tallulah's saying to Herman as he rose to go, "Wait a minute, darling, just wait a minute. I have something to show you." She threw aside the sheets, pointed down at the naked, miserable Emery and said, "Just tell me, darling, if you've ever seen a prick that big." I don't know what Herman said, but it must have been pleasant because there was no fight that night, nothing to predict what was to come.

I still have a diary entry, written a few days later, asking myself whether talk about the size of the male organ isn't a homosexual preoccupation: if things aren't too bad in other ways I doubt if any woman cares very much. Almost certainly Tallulah didn't care about the size or the function: it was the stylish, *épater* palaver of her day.

It is a mark of many famous people that they cannot part with their brightest hour: what worked once must always work. Tallulah had been the nineteen-twenties' most daring girl, but what had been dashing, even brave, had become by 1939 shrill and tiring. The life of the special darlings in the world of art and society had been made old-fashioned by the economic miseries of those who had never been darlings. Nothing is displaced on a single day and much was left over during the Depression, but the train had made a sharp historical swing and the fashionable folk, their life and customs, had become loud and tacky.

Tallulah, in the first months of the play, gave a fine performance, had a well-deserved triumph. It was sad to watch it all decline into high-jinks on the stage and in life. Long before her death, beginning with my play, I think, she threw the talent around to amuse the campy boys who came each opening night to watch her vindicate their view of women. I didn't clearly understand all that when I first met her, but I knew that while there was probably not more than five years' difference in our ages, and a bond in our Southern background — her family came from an Alabama town close to my mother's — we were a generation apart. I first realized it when we were still in rehearsal, about a week before the play was to open in Baltimore.

Tallulah, Herman and I were having dinner in the old Artists and Writers Club, a hangout for newspapermen. Tallulah took two small bottles from her pocketbook, put them on the table, and seemed to forget about them. As we were about to go back to rehearsal, she picked up one bottle and tipped it to put drops in her eyes. She rose from the table, repacked the bottles, led the way to the door, and let out a shriek that brought the restaurant to its feet. Herman rushed to her, she pushed him aside, other people pushed toward her, she turned for the door, changed her mind, and whispered to nobody, "I have put the wrong drops in my eyes." Herman ran to a phone booth, she shouted after him, he called out that he was getting a doctor, she said he was to mind his business, and suddenly, in the shouting and running, she grabbed my arm, pulled me into the toilet and said, "Get Herman off that phone. I put the cocaine in my eyes and I don't tell that to doctors or to anybody else. Tell him to shut up about it or I won't go back to the theatre." She sat down at a table, grinned at everybody, and ordered herself a shot of whiskey. I squeezed my way into the phone booth, told Herman about the cocaine. He moved slowly toward her and said, "Put down the whiskey and come outside."

On the sidewalk he said, "I don't like what just happened. This play is going to open on time and I want you to cut the nonsense."

Tallulah said, in controlled stage-anger, "I'm a professional. It's none of your damn business what I do. I warn you never to talk to me this way again."

As she hailed a taxi, Herman said, "If you don't come back to rehearsals in half an hour, don't come back at all." She slammed the door of the taxi, he and I walked back to the theatre, and ten minutes later Tallulah appeared on the stage.

Cocaine was not mentioned again until the opening night party she gave in her Baltimore hotel rooms. It was, indeed, quite a night. Her father, the Speaker of the House of Representatives, and her uncle, the Senator, had come down from Washington. Hammett had arrived a few days before, then Dorothy Parker and her husband Alan Campbell, with Sara and Gerald Murphy. We were a mixed bag, the cast and guests, trying to circulate in a room too small for us.

With time and booze things got loud and the Senator took to singing "Dixie," spirituals, and a Civil War song, until the fastidious Gerald Murphy said to him, "Lovely. But now you must rest your fine vocal cords."

Tallulah was sitting in a large group giving the monologue she always thought was conversation. I was tired, waiting to go to my room, and I guess I yawned once too often because she began to tease me, in the kind of nagging fashion she used when she knew somebody wanted to leave her. A young Negro waiter moved back and forth, passing drinks, and as he came near us she asked him if he wanted to sleep with her or me. He stood still, frightened. She pulled him toward her and kissed him.

I said to the waiter, "Better get out of here now. She's probably not up to much, but this is Maryland."

He went rapidly toward the door, Tallulah went after him, offering to hit me along the way, and Hammett moved behind her. When things had settled down, she put her arms around Hammett and promised that she'd forgive him because she was a sucker for a handsome man. He thanked her and said he didn't much like to be around people who took dope, in his Pinkerton days he had been more afraid of them than of murderers. They talked that over for a while but I lost track until I heard her shout at him, "You don't know what you are talking about. I tell you cocaine isn't habit-forming and I know because I've been taking it for years."

When I laughed too long she got upset with me

again and Gerald Murphy said he thought I'd be safer in bed.

Unfortunately my bedroom was next door and I lay sleepless until five in the morning. Then I fell asleep to be awakened by a fight that was going on behind my bed. Tallulah and a woman I had met at the party — an assistant or an ex-secretary — were arguing about an income tax claim and what the woman had done with Tallulah's money. (I think that several years later there was a lawsuit between them.) I yelled through the door that I wanted to sleep. Insults came back and then a demand to join them for a drink. When I said I didn't want a drink and why didn't they go knock each other off the hotel roof, one of them began to pound on my door with what sounded like a bottle and, in time, the pounding became, with giggles, the rhythm of "America the Beautiful." I got dressed and decided to go sit in the park, but before I left the room I broke a desk chair against their door.

Tallulah sent commands the next day for me to appear at rehearsals and apologize, but I was with Dottie, Alan and the Murphys in the hotel dining room from ten in the morning until they closed the place at midnight. It was one of the most pleasant days of my life. I was sleepy and content: the play had gotten fine reviews, we all had a lot to drink, and nobody talked about the play or the theatre. I remember dozing on the table for a while and waking to hear Gerald say, "It's not an easy business, the theatre," and Dottie's saying, "Lilly does things the hard way. Why didn't she have sense enough to get Harpo Marx instead of Tallulah?" and then a long discussion about General Sherman, who was Sara Murphy's grandfather.

There are not many good critics for any art, but there have been almost none for the modern theatre. The intellectuals among them know little about an operating theatre and the middlebrows look at plays as if they were at a race track for the morning line-up. It is a mixed-up picture in many ways. One critic who wrote that *The Little Foxes* was a febrile play later called it an American classic without explaining why he changed his mind.

The *New York Times*, for many years, has been the only newspaper that mattered to the success of a play. That is not the fault of the paper, but it is not a good state for a struggling art form. Now, with Mr. Clive Barnes, even that has changed for the worse: a good review by him no longer makes a hit, but a bad review does damage. The *Times* has had a long list of earnest, honest, undistinguished critics. Walter Kerr is the only one, I think, who learned and thrived. Mr. Barnes is the first fashion-swinger in the list but, like most, he can't quite find where the swing is located for the new season.

I knew many of the virtues and the mistakes of *The Little Foxes* before the play opened. I wanted, I needed an interesting critical mind to tell what I had done beyond the limited amount I could see for myself. But the high praise and the reservations seemed

to me stale stuff and I think were one of the reasons
the great success of the play sent me into a wasteful,
ridiculous depression. I sat drinking for months
after the play opened trying to figure out what I had
wanted to say and why some of it got lost.

I grew restless, sickish, digging around the random
memories that had been the conscious, semiconscious
material for the play. I had meant to half-mock my
own youthful high-class innocence in Alexandra, the
young girl in the play; I had meant people to smile
at, and to sympathize with, the sad, weak Birdie, certainly I had not meant them to cry; I had meant the
audience to recognize some part of themselves in the
money-dominated Hubbards; I had not meant people
to think of them as villains to whom they had no
connection.

I belonged, on my mother's side, to a banking,
storekeeping family from Alabama and Sunday dinners were large, with four sisters and three brothers
of my grandmother's generation, their children, and a
few cousins of my age. These dinners were long, with
high-spirited talk and laughter from the older people
of who did what to whom, what good nigger had con-
sented to thirty percent interest on his cotton crop and
what bad nigger had made a timid protest, what new
white partner had been outwitted, what benefits the
year had brought from the Southern business interests
they had left behind for the Northern profits they had
had sense enough to move toward.

When I was fourteen, in one of my many religious

periods, I yelled across that Sunday's dinner table at a great-aunt, "You have a spatulate face made to dig in the mud for money. May God forgive you."

My aunt rose, came around the table and slapped me with her napkin. I said, "Someday I'll pay you back unless the dear God helps me conquer the evil spirit of revenge," and ran from the room as my gentle mother started to cry. But later that night, she knocked on my locked door and said that if I came out I could have a squab for dinner. My father was out of New York but, evidently informed of the drama by my mother, wrote to me saying that he hoped I had sense enough not to revenge myself until I was as tall and as heavy as my great-aunt.

But a few years after I had stopped being pleased with the word spatulate, a change occurred for which even now I have no explanation: I began to think that greed and the cheating that is its usual companion were comic as well as evil and I began to like the family dinners with the talk of who did what to whom. I particularly looked forward to the biannual dinner when the sisters and brothers assembled to draw lots for "the diamond" that had been left, almost thirty years before, in my great-grandmother's estate. Sometimes they would use the length of a strip of paper to designate the winner, sometimes the flip of a coin, and once I was allowed to choose a number up to eight and the correct guesser was to get the diamond. But nobody, as far as I knew, ever did get it. No sooner was the winner declared than one or the other would sulk and, by prearrangement, another loser would console the sulker, and a third would start the real event of the afternoon: an open charge of cheating. The paper, the coin, my number, all had been fixed or tampered with. That was wild and funny. Funnier because my mother's generation would sit white-faced, sometimes tearful, appalled at what was happening, all of them envying the vigor of their parents, half knowing that they were broken spirits who wished the world was nicer, but who were still so anxious to inherit the money that they made no protest.

I was about eighteen when my great-uncle Jake took the dinner hours to describe how he and a new partner had bought a street of slum houses in downtown New York. He, Jake, during a lunch break in the signing of the partnership, removed all the toilet seats from the buildings and sold them for fifty dollars. But, asked my mother's cousin, what will the poor people who live there do without toilet seats? "Let us," said Jake, "approach your question in a practical manner. I ask you to accompany me now to the bathroom, where I will explode my bowels in the manner of the impoverished and you will see for yourself how it is done." As he reached for her hand to lead her to the exhibition, my constantly ailing cousin began to cry in high, long sounds. Her mother said to her, "Go along immediately with your Uncle Jake. You are being disrespectful to him."

I guess all that was the angry comedy I wanted to mix with the drama.

Angry comedy came another way. I was to get my first taste during *The Little Foxes* of the red-baiting that later turned my life into disorder and financial disaster.

The Spanish Civil War — I had been in Spain during the war — had reached the sad day of Franco's victory and many Republicans were trapped on what was known as the International Bridge. Some of them were my friends, some of them I only knew about. Their lives were at stake. Many of us sent all the money we could give or collect and looked around to find other money fast. Herman Shumlin and I decided to ask the cast of *The Little Foxes* if they would do a benefit for the Spanish refugees. Tallulah and the rest of the cast were courteous but well within their rights when they refused, and nothing more was said about benefits until the week after Russia moved into Finland.

I had been in Helsinki in 1937 for two weeks and had turned my head each day from the giant posters of Hitler pasted to the side wall of my hotel. One night a member of our Olympic team, a man of Finnish descent, had taken me to a large rally of Hitler sympathizers and translated for me their admiring speeches. I needed no translator for the raised arms, the cheers, the Wessel song.

Finland's ambassador to Washington was a handsome and charming man who met Tallulah at a dinner party. The day following Tallulah's meeting with the ambassador she announced that *The Little Foxes* would give a benefit for the Finnish refugees. The day following that Shumlin and I announced that *The Little Foxes* would not give a benefit. I can't remember now whether we explained that we had been refused a benefit for Spain, but I do remember that suddenly what had been no more than a theatre fight turned into a political attack: it was made to seem that we agreed with the invasion of Finland, refused aid to true democrats, were, ourselves, dangerous Communists. It was my first experience of such goings-on and I didn't have sense enough to know that Tallulah's press statements, so much better than ours, or more in tune with the times, were being guided by the expert ambassador. Although her anger — she often had the righteousness that belongs to a certain kind of aging sinner — once aroused needed no guidance and stood up well against all reason. And nobody has ever been able to control me when I feel that I have been treated unjustly. I am, in fact, bewildered by all injustice, at first certain that it cannot be, then shocked into rigidity, then obsessed, and finally as certain as a Grand Inquisitor that God wishes me to move ahead, correct and holy. Through those days Tallulah and I were, indeed, a pair.

And so we never spoke again for almost thirty years. Then I met her at a party and heard myself say, "Maybe it's time we said hello." The face that looked up from years of physical and spiritual beatings was blank. I said, "I'm Lillian Hellman," and Tallulah flew toward me in a scream of good-natured greetings and a holiday of kisses. I was pleased for the first half-hour. But reconciliations can be as noisy as the fights that caused them.

Only two diaries written at the end of 1938 could convince me now that *Watch on the Rhine* came out of Henry James, although, of course, seeds in the wind, the long journey they make, their crosses and mutations, is not a new story for writers and even make you hope that your seeds may scatter for those to come.

I was driving back to the farm trying not to listen to the noise that came from two crates of Pekin ducks when I began to think of James's *The American* and *The Europeans.* In the short time since James, the United States had become the dominant country not alone in money and power, but in imposing on other people a morality which was designed in part to hide its self-interest. Was that a new American game or had we learned it from the English who invented it to hold down their lower classes? We still spoke as nineteenth-century Cromwellians in church, home, and university, but increasingly, the more we recognized disorder and corruption at home the more insistent we grew about national purity.

Many Europeans had moved here with the triumph of Hitler in the 1930's. Few of us asked questions about their past or present convictions because we took for granted that they had left either in fear of persecution or to make a brave protest. They were our kind of folks. It took me a long time to find out that many of them had strange histories and that their hosts, or the people who vouched for them, knew all about their past. Two of the perhaps eight or nine that I met turned out to have unexpected reasons for emigration: both had been Nazi sympathizers; in one case, the grandfather wanted to preserve his remarkable art collection from the threatening sounds the "new barbarians" made about modern painting; in the other, bribe money had not been able to suppress a nineteenth-century conversion from Judaism to Luther. I was vaguely related to that family, and when I asked about the truth of the rumor, the son of the family never spoke to me again. But a few weeks later I had a note from his mother saying that she was surprised to find that certain Jews in America claimed a blood connection to her family, when, in fact, they had "no legal or moral right" to do so. I had no right, from my safe place, to feel bitter about such people, but I did and, of course, by 1938 I had been through the life and death of my friend Julia, and had been to Spain during the Civil War, and had been moved by men willing to die for what they believed in.

I wanted to write a play about nice, liberal Americans whose lives would be shaken up by Europeans, by a world the new Fascists had won because the old values had long been dead. I put the play in a small Ohio town. That didn't work at all. Then one night, coming out of a long dream about the streets of London, I knew that I had stubbornly returned to the people and the place of *Days to Come.* I was obsessed with my dream, stopped writing for a month or so, and only started again when I found the root of the dream; then I moved the play to Washington, placed it in the house of a rich, liberal family who were about to meet their anti-fascist son-in-law, a German, who had fought in Spain. He was, of course, a form of Julia.

The dream had taken me back to an evening in 1936 when, on a visit to London, I had a phone call from the famous Margot Asquith. I had never met Lady Asquith, but I remembered Dorothy Parker writing of her *Autobiography*, "The affair between Margot Asquith and Margot Asquith will live as one of the prettiest love stories in all literature." Lady Asquith told me that the novelist Charles Morgan wanted to meet me, would I come to dinner? It was a strange evening: from the minute the butler opened the Baker Street door and said, "Oh, you're bloody *young,*" I felt as if I had gone swimming in strong waters and would have to struggle hard to reach land again.

The dinner party was Lady Asquith, her son Anthony, a movie director, her daughter Elizabeth, Princess Bibesco, and the Romanian Prince Antoine Bibesco, her husband. Princess Bibesco had written a number of books and I would have liked to talk to her, being at that point in my life most respectful of lady-books that carried delicate overtones of sadness. There was no Charles Morgan and Lady Asquith was surprised that I thought there would be, but halfway through the dinner a very tall young man sat down next to me and, although I never heard his name through the marshmallow English syllables, there was some reference to his royal cousins.

Tony Asquith was most pleasant, but his mother frowned at me down the table as if she didn't understand why I was there and, as far as I remember, Prince Bibesco said no word. The butlers were plentiful, the conversation so faltering that one had the impression that everybody was ill, and when Bibesco rose, pushed aside his plate, said he'd meet us upstairs, I thought only that he was a sensible man to refuse the bad food.

When we left the savories — that upper-class English habit of drowning the bad with the worse — we joined the prince in a small room off the drawing room. It was filled by a large poker table, the chips already racked, and Bibesco didn't look up from his game of solitaire. Lady Asquith said she was due at a Parliamentary committee, called me Mrs. Dillman as she said goodbye, and left the rest of us to watch the prince play solitaire. When his third game came out fine, he patted me on the arm and asked if I played poker. I said yes, I liked it; he said he did, too, but didn't play much anymore and was out of practice. The semiroyal gentleman coughed, but I thought that was because a Mr. and Mrs. Something-or-Other came into the room.

In a few minutes we were all in a poker game. Elizabeth Bibesco didn't play but sat reading in a room off our room. In the first half-hour of the game her husband made jokes about how you cut cards, in what direction you started dealing, did a straight come before a full house, and by midnight I had lost almost three hundred pounds and semiroyalty had lost over five hundred pounds. I have no memory of what happened to the two strangers: I think they lost or won very little, although the man sneezed a lot through the evening. By the time I decided that my losses were far more than I could afford, I had learned that Bibesco had been the Romanian ambassador to Washington and a regular at the games of Vice-President Charles Curtis, a famous poker player. And I had heard enough to understand that it was not my literary reputation that had gone ahead of me, but a piece in the *New York Herald Tribune* saying that the boys in the famous New York Thanatopsis poker game had thought of inviting me to join them, but finally decided a woman would set a bad precedent. This was verified by the royal cousin, who drove me to my hotel in a high-powered racing car. He was a charming mixture of glum and glee as he said that he knew he was a bad player, always vowed he'd never go back to that particular high-stake game, and went back whenever he was asked. I thought about that poker game for years afterward and came to feel that the evening, the dinner, Bibesco, and Lady Asquith herself were characters sitting in a second-act drawing room because the stagehands had forgotten to tell them that the scenery had changed to the edge of a volcano.

It was a pleasant experience, *Watch on the Rhine*. There are plays that, whatever their worth, come along at the right time, and the right time is the essence of the theatre and the cinema. From the first day of rehearsal things went well. It was a hardworking cast of nice people, with the exception of Paul Lukas, the best actor among them; but his capers were open and comic. (He told me that he had been a trusted follower of the Hungarian Communist Béla Kun, but that the week before Kun fell he had joined Kun's enemies. He saw nothing contradictory in now playing a self-sacrificing anti-Fascist.) But not everybody thought Paul was funny. John Lodge, then an actor and later to be our ambassador to Spain — when Dorothy Parker heard about his diplomatic appointment she said, "Lilly, let us, as patriots, join hands and walk into the water" — was shocked when Paul cheated him at tennis, and Eric Roberts, who played Paul's twelve-year-old son, disliked him so much that some nights he ate garlic before he climbed into Paul's lap and other nights he rubbed his hair with foul-smelling whale oil. I remember all that with pleasure, although a diary tells me that Herman Shumlin and I were having our usual fights.

The Baltimore opening of *Watch on the Rhine* went just fine and gave me a chance to see the medical historian Dr. Henry Sigerist. Sigerist was one of the heroes of my life: a learned man in medicine who read in many other fields; a political radical who was an

expert cook and on whose judgment professional tea
and wine tasters often depended; a tough man who
was gentle; a sad man who did not complain. And
he was a wise political observer: he had left the University of Leipzig, guessing two years before Hitler
came to power what was to come, and several years
before the full flower of Joe McCarthy, during a time
when the rest of us thought McCarthy a clown, he re-
signed from Johns Hopkins University and moved
back to his native Switzerland.

The week before he left America he came to visit
us at the Pleasantville farm and cooked a great and
complicated meal with our friend Gregory Zilboorg,
and all of us were happy with food and wine and
affection.

I was to see him only once again after that dinner,
in 1953, when, because he believed that McCarthy
might use him against me — I had the year before
been called before the House Un-American Activities
Committee and that year been subpoenaed by a summons that was never served by the McCarthy committee — if I came to visit him and his wife in Switzerland, we arranged to meet in Milan.

It was fine that day in Milan. Henry had gone to
school there and now had pleasure in showing it to
me. We drove a long way to a monastery that had
remarkable early wall paintings and the abbot and
two old priests were openly admiring of this Marxist
unbeliever; we drove further to a small castle on a
hill where the owner, a young woman, had a Cana-

letto he wanted to see again and they talked together of her grandparents; we had lunch and dinner in small, fine restaurants where the owners knew Sigerist and one of them asked for his opinion of a new wine and neither would allow him to pay a bill; we toured the ugly Milan Cathedral and he told me of the difference in the history of the Northern and Southern Catholic Churches; and when we said goodbye he told me he was ill and that I must come back soon because he would have only a few years more to see his friends.

He died on time, as he did everything else.

It is the lifelong problem of only children that they doubt all affection that is offered, even that which has been proved, and so, as the years passed, I told myself that Sigerist had been polite and kind to me, but that I had not gone back to see him because I was not needed or wanted. I only recognized the vanity behind my lack of vanity when his daughter published a part of his diary in which there is proof of what he felt for me. We all have been spared some nonsense and I have been spared caring very much what most people thought about me. But I cared so much for what this distinguished man thought that I cut the words from the book, put them in a frame, and locked the frame in a safe.

Yesterday, nineteen years later, standing in a pretty Wellfleet cemetery at Edmund Wilson's funeral, I thought of Henry Sigerist and knew why. These two men, so different in temperament, in interests, in belief, one so European, one so American, were alike in the kind of wide-ranging mind rare in a time of specialists, alike in the nineteenth-century conviction that culture was applied curiosity. I remembered once telling Edmund that I had asked Sigerist if it was true that he knew thirteen languages and he had said, "No, no. I know only nine. I can read in three others but I cannot say more than a sentence and that not well." Edmund had smiled at that, but a few minutes later told me that he was studying Hungarian and I knew my story had started a charming competitiveness in him and a counting on his fingers.

Watch on the Rhine is the only play I have ever written that came out in one piece, as if I had seen a landscape and never altered the trees or the seasons of their colors. All other work for me had been fragmented, hunting in an open field with shot from several guns, following the course but unable to see clearly, recovering the shot hands full, then hands empty from stumbling and spilling. But here, for the first and last time, the work I did, the actors, the rehearsals, the success of the play, even the troubles that I have forgotten, make a pleasant oneness and have been lost to the past. The real memories of that time are not for the play but for the people who passed through the time of it. President Roosevelt was one of them.

In those days it was a yearly custom for a play to be chosen to give a kind of command performance before the President for the benefit of the Infantile Paralysis Fund. When *Watch on the Rhine* was invited to Washington for a Sunday night early in 1942, it was the first public appearance of President Roosevelt since war had been declared.

John Lodge was a Naval Reserve officer about to be called up, and a good deal of the train ride from New York to Washington was taken up with the question of what he should wear to the White House for a supper party after the performance. A Navy uniform seemed premature; others of us argued that plain dinner clothes were not quite right for a man of distinguished family about to serve his country, perhaps to die. I suggested a sword and red ribbon as being neither too little nor too much, but John, who seemed to like that idea, said it would be impossible because nobody could find such stuff on a Sunday.

While the cast rehearsed light cues and tried the acoustics of the theatre, I talked an idle assistant manager into phoning a friend who worked at a theatre warehouse and offering him fifty bucks if he could come up with sword and wide ribbon. In a few hours I was backstage ironing the old crushed ribbon and clanking around with the sword. I guess people laughed too much because John, who had seemed most pleased about the idea, now refused the sword in peevish, stiff terms. I felt bad about that, it would have been nice, and only came around to feeling better when Mr. Roosevelt entered the theatre. The bold, handsome head had so much intelligence and confidence that the wheelchair in which he sat seemed not a handicap but an interesting way to move about.

At supper Roosevelt remembered that I had once visited him at Warm Springs, coming, by accident, on the same day as Huey Long. We talked about Long and my native Louisiana, but he was more interested — he asked me several times — in when I had written *Watch on the Rhine*. When I told him I started it a year and a half before the war, he shook his head and said in that case he didn't understand why Morris Ernst, the lawyer, had told him that I was so opposed to the war that I had paid for the "Communist" war protesters who kept a continuous picket line around the White House before Germany attacked the Soviet Union. I said I didn't know Mr. Ernst's reasons for that nonsense story, but Ernst's family had been in business with my Alabama family long ago and that wasn't a good mark on any man. Mr. Roosevelt laughed and said he'd enjoy passing that message on to Mr. Ernst.

But the story about my connection with the picket line was there to stay, often repeated when the red-baiting days reached hurricane force. But by that time, some of the pleasant memories of *Watch on the Rhine* had also disappeared: Lukas, once so loud in gratitude for the play, put in his frightened, blunted knife for a newspaper interviewer, and Lucille Watson, a remarkable actress, changed her written affection for me when she came to work in *The Autumn Garden* almost ten years later. She rehearsed with us then for three days. On the fourth day she did not return. She told another actor that perhaps she could put up with me because I was "a toilet-trained Jew," but she couldn't put up with Harold Clurman, the director, because he was "just plain Jew." The hardest lesson to learn in the theatre is to take nobody too seriously.

It is possible that because the war so drastically changed the world, the small, less observed things changed without being recognized. Now, looking back, I think that after *Watch on the Rhine* much of the pleasant high-jinks of the theatre were never to be seen again because the theatre, like the rest of the country, became expensive, earnest and conservative. The Tallulahs and the Lukases were not easy to take, but they belonged to a time I liked better. Whatever the reason, the theatre pictures behind my eyes for the period after that are fragmented and it would be useless and untruthful for me to order them up from scrapbooks or other people's memories. About the plays that followed that period, the pictures are there, but not many are much more than a camera angle that was part of a whole, of course, but is now seen only by itself.

Of *The Searching Wind* I have very little now except the memory of a wonderful old actor, Dudley Digges, arriving at seven-thirty each night during the run of the play to meet Montgomery Clift, a gifted, inexperienced young actor in his first large part. To-

gether they would sit on the stage until the second curtain call and go through a scene from Shakespeare or
Ibsen or Chekhov, or a series of poems, anything that
Digges had chosen to teach Monty. It was mighty nice,
the two of them, and I took to going to the theatre
several times a week just to stand in the wings and
watch the delicate relationship between the dedicated
old and the dedicated young. I was never to see much
of Clift after the closing of the play, but in the years
that followed, mostly unhappy ones for him, I am told,
I would often get a long-distance call from him, we
would arrange to meet, never manage it, but always
we would talk of Dudley Digges, who died a few years
after *The Searching Wind.*

I had always planned *The Little Foxes* as a trilogy,
knowing that I had jumped into the middle of the life
of the Hubbards and would want to go forward in
time. But in 1946 it seemed right to go back to their
youth, their father and mother, to the period of the
Civil War. I believed that I could now make clear
that I had meant the first play as a kind of satire. I
tried to do that in *Another Part of The Forest,* but
what I thought funny or outrageous the critics thought
straight stuff; what I thought was bite they thought
sad, touching, or plotty and melodramatic. Perhaps,
as one critic said, I blow a stage to pieces without
knowing it. In any case, I had a good time directing
the play, not because I wanted to, but because I was
tired of arguments and knew no director I thought
was right for me. I did a good job, I think, so good

that I fooled myself into thinking I was a director, a mistake that I was to discover a few years later. But then and now it gives me pleasure that I found an unknown girl, Patricia Neal, and watched her develop into a good actress and a remarkable woman.

With *Montserrat,* an adaptation I made from the French play by Emmanuel Roblès, I not only cast the play with a kind of abandoned belief that good actors can play anything, but I directed it in a fumbling, frightened way, intimidated by Emlyn Williams, the British actor and writer, who was playing the leading part. I do not blame Mr. Williams for his disapproval of me, although the way he showed it had a bad effect on the actors and thus on the play. He must have known from the first days of rehearsal that fear infects and corrupts what it touches. It is best in the theatre to act with confidence no matter how little right you have to it. It is a special and valuable gift, directing, but it has come to its present power mostly in comedies or musicals. Few dramas can stand up against another assertive talent, even if it is more distinguished than the original creator. Movies have come close to solving that problem: the director and writer are now often the same person, or two people who seen to function as one. But in the theatre, drama, even plain, dull seriousness, is still a business of unsolved delicacy between the writer, the director and the actors.

*   *   *

Many writers work best in time of trouble: no money, the cold outside and in, even sickness and the end in view. But I have always known that when trouble comes I must face it fast and move with speed, even though the speed is thoughtless and sometimes damaging. For such impatient people, calm is necessary for hard work — long days, months of fiddling is the best way of life.

I wrote *The Autumn Garden* in such a period. I was at a good age; I lived on a farm that was, finally, running fine and I knew I had found the right place to live for the rest of my life. Hammett and I were both making a lot of money, and not caring about where it went was fun. We had been together almost twenty years, some of them bad, a few of them shabby, but now we had both stopped drinking and the early excited years together had settled into a passionate affection so unexpected to both of us that we were as shy and careful with each other as courting children. Without words, we knew that we had survived for the best of all reasons, the pleasure of each other.

I could not wait to hear what he thought about the news in the morning paper, about a book, a departing guest, a day's hunt for birds and rabbits, an hour's walk in the woods. And nobody in my life has ever been as anxious to have me stay in a room, talk late into the night, get up in the morning. I guess it was the best time for me, certainly the best time of our life together. Now, I think, that somewhere we both knew — the signs were already there, Joe McCarthy was over the land — that we had to make it good because it had to end. One year later Hammett was in jail; two years later the place where I intended to live the rest of my life had to be sold; three or four years later neither of us had any money and, more important than any of that, all of which can be borne without too much trouble, we were to face Hammett's death around every corner. If we did smell the future, I am glad we had sense enough never to mention it.

I have many times written about Dash's pleasure in *The Autumn Garden*. Now, this minute, I can hear myself laugh at the fierce, angry manner in which he spoke his praise, as if he hated the words, was embarrassed by them. He was forever after defensive — he had never been about my work or his — if anybody had any reservations about the play. A short time after the play opened, I came home very pleased to tell him that Norman Mailer had told me how good he thought the play. Norman had said it was very good, could have been great, but I had lost my nerve.

Dash said, "Almost everybody loses their nerve. You almost didn't, and that's what counts, and what he should have said."

By 1955 I needed money. I wish I could tell myself that was why I adapted Jean Anouilh's *The Lark*. But my reason was not money: I was feeling mischievous and the reasons for the mischief still exist as they were written on a Ritz Hotel menu in London.

My producer, Kermit Bloomgarden, had bought the

play and wanted me to make a new adaptation. I flew
to London to see Christopher Fry's version, didn't like
it, cabled Kermit that it wasn't up my alley. Then I
had lunch at the Ritz with Dr. Van Loewen, Anouilh's
agent. I was pleased to meet a doctor-agent having
only once before heard of one, Milton Bender, a
former dentist, who perhaps had a better right to the
title. So I said, "I am sorry, Doctor, but I do not
believe this play is right for me. I . . ."

The doctor said, "We, Mr. Anouilh and I, have the
greatest respect for your gifts, Mrs. Hellman, but
L'Alouette comes from the mind of a poet and must,
therefore, be adapted by a poet."

"Poet," I said, "*poet?*"

"We have the greatest respect for your gifts, Mrs.
Hellman, but . . ."

"You are right. I am not a poet."

"There," he said. "You are a lady of honesty for
whose gifts we have . . ."

"You don't need a poet. You need George Bernard
Shaw, but he's dead."

The doctor said, "Shaw was not a poet. I do not
think he would have been the right adaptor, either."

After I made that note on my menu and thought
about foreigners, I said, "Mr. Shaw wrote a fine play
about Joan of Arc, without all of Mr. Anouilh's bubble
glory stuff."

"Mr. Anouilh is a poet," said the doctor.

"Perhaps," I said, "but not in French," laughed,
and felt ashamed of myself.

I don't remember how long it took Bloomgarden to talk me out of the conversation with the doctor, but by the time I agreed to do the play I was convinced that Joan was history's first modern career girl, wise, unattractive in what she knew about the handling of men, straight out of a woman's magazine. The wonderful story lay, as Shaw had seen it, in the miraculous self-confidence that carried defeated men into battle against all sense and reason, forced a pious girl into a refusal of her church, caused the terrible death that still has to do with the rest of us, forever, wherever her name is heard.

And so for good or bad, I scaled down the play, cut the comparisons to the World War II German invasion of France and the tributes to the French spirit. I had doubts about the French spirit and, if the gossip about Mr. Anouilh has any truth, he had doubts; and I didn't like fake doves flying out over the audience to show the soaring spirit of Joan, the victory of idealism, or just to indicate the end of a play. And the fine, straightforward performance of Julie Harris helped make the play the first success Mr. Anouilh had in America, which is possibly why we never again heard from him or from the doctor, although all profits, quite properly, have been accepted by them.

Some kind of confidence, even fake, is needed for any work, but it is particularly required in the theatre, where ordinary timidity and stumbling seem like disintegration, and are infectious and corruptive to other frightened people. I think now that I began to leave the theatre with the production of *Candide,* an operetta with music by Leonard Bernstein, lyrics by Richard Wilbur. (I was not to leave for another two plays, but I am slow at leaving anything.)

I can account for the deterioration of my script from what I think was good to what I know is not good, but any such account would be confused, full of those miserable, small complaints and blames that mean nothing except to the person making them. I was not used to collaboration, I had become, with time, too anxious to stay out of fights, and because I was working with people who knew more about the musical theatre than I did, I took suggestions and made changes that I didn't believe in, tried making them with speed I cannot manage.

All that, I could and did put aside. The confidence went for another reason: I knew we were in bad trouble the day the cast first read and sang the play. I knew it, I said it, and yet I sat scared, inwardly raging, outwardly petty passive before the great talents of Leonard Bernstein, who knew about music, and Tyrone Guthrie, the director, who knew about the theatre. The lady producer knew nothing about either.

All of it, after the nice, hopeful period of work with Lennie and Richard Wilbur, through rehearsals to the closing night of *Candide* — and again, years later, the 1972 Kennedy Center revival with which I refused any connection — was sad and wasteful and did not need to be.

Several months after the play closed in New York, Tony Guthrie said, "Lennie, Wilbur, Oliver Smith, Irene Sharaff, Miss Hellman and Mr. Guthrie were too much talent for a good brew." That is hard for me to believe. Vanity, which I think is what he meant, can be of great use: it was dangerous during *Candide* because it was on a blind rampage.

I think now that Guthrie was as frightened as I was. I should have recognized that the night of the Boston dress rehearsal when Marc Blitzstein, an old friend of Lennie's and mine, walked me back to the hotel. We were depressed, neither of us talked the long way across the Boston Common. At the door of my room Marc said, "You're cooked, kid, and so is the show. I was sitting near Guthrie. He grinned at me once, his mouth full of sandwich and wine, and said, 'Well, Marc, that's that. Lillian is often right, but Lennie is so charming.'"

Guthrie was an imaginative man, bold in a timid business, uncaring about money in a world that cared about little else. It is true that the imagination led to tinkering: he reinterpreted almost every play he directed, but he did it with brilliance.

I turn my head now, look out at a jetty in front of my house, and see again this giant-tall man sitting on the end rock, telling me of his childhood, his university days, and then, as if he had talked more than he meant, suddenly pitching himself into the water at a dangerous angle. In the years after *Candide*, we sometimes saw each other, more often wrote letters. In one letter, I told him that *Candide* had done bad things to me, I wasn't working. He did not answer that letter, but a few months later he was in New York and we met for lunch. As I came in the restaurant door, a voice on my right side said, "Stop the nonsense. Get on with new work, get on with it today."

It was a valuable accident that a few days after that, or so I thought until a week ago, I spent the evening with Elena and Edmund Wilson. During the evening we talked of a man we both knew and Edmund asked why he didn't write anymore. I mumbled something about writing blocks, I had one myself, all of us, and so on.

Edmund said, "Foolishness. A writer writes. That's all there is to it."

For anybody of my generation, so eager for the neurosis, yours if you could manage it, if desperate somebody else's, the hardheaded sense of that was good stuff. But it did not happen a few days after I saw Guthrie. Last week I came back from Edmund's funeral and sat thinking about him most of the night. The next morning I went through old diaries of the many times I had spent with the Wilsons and found that "A writer writes. That's all there is to it," came almost two years after my lunch with Guthrie. But it is true that the next day after Edmund said it I went to work on *Toys in the Attic*.

Months before that day, Hammett and I had walked down from the house into the beach grass to look at a quail nest and see how things were going. I had known about the emphysema since Dash got out of the Army in 1945, known it had grown worse when he went to jail in 1951, knew that we could go less and less to the beach or any place else. But I don't think I had ever heard the heavy panting breath until that day as we climbed the steps back to the house. He stopped and lowered his head. I held out a hand.

He looked away from my hand and said, "I've been meaning to tell you. There's this man. Other people, people who say they love him, want him to make good, be rich. So he does it for them and finds they don't like him that way, so he fucks it up, and comes out worse than before. Think about it."

I wrote an act and a half and gave it to Hammett to read. When he had finished with it, he said, "Take the boat and go fishing. Forget the play for today. Maybe by night I'll . . ."

"No," I said. "This time you don't have to tell me what's wrong. I can write about men, but I can't write a play that centers on a man. I've got to tear it up, make it about the women around him, his sisters, his bride, her mother and — "

"Well," he said, "then my idea's out the window. Never mind. I'll use it myself someday."

He never lived to use it. But he lived long enough to have great pleasure from the play, and the last trip he ever made was to Boston for the opening. We had fun together, very like the old, first days of jokes, and wanting to be together, resenting the times we weren't. I skipped rehearsals for a couple of days and we went once more to see Paul Revere's house, Faneuil Hall, the Old South Meeting House, drove out to the Old Manse in Concord and had an argument about Emerson as if we had never had it before. I realized that in the pleasure of those days I had forgotten how sick he was and was worried that he would pay for the tramping about. But for the first time in years he seemed better for it, and we had late, cheerful dinners in our rooms.

I said, "The Ritz Hotel has the best thermoses. I wish I could just up and take one home."

"For years you've thought you were stealing what hotels mean for you to take, washrags, shoeshine cloths, soap, and then patting yourself on the back for the nerve of doing it. Take the thermos. You'll feel better."

"I can't. And you've never stolen anything."

"I never wanted anything enough."

"That isn't the reason. You think it isn't dignified."

The next day, coming back from a shopping trip with Maureen Stapleton during which I persuaded her into two expensive dresses and an alligator bag about which to this day, whenever there is too much of what she calls wine, she says I bankrupted her forever, Hammett was waiting for me with his suitcase packed.

I said, "You didn't tell me you were leaving today."

He said, "Did we ever tell each other?"

(This morning, twelve years later, I poured myself a cup of coffee from a Ritz Hotel thermos bottle. Dash had put it on top of his clothes, sent for a bellboy to close the valise, and winked at me when the bellboy showed no sign of seeing the thermos. No, I told myself this morning, we had never told each other, never made a plan, and yet we had moved a number of times from West Coast to East Coast, bought and sold three houses, been well-heeled and broke, parted, come together, and never had plans or even words for the future. In my case, I think, the mixture of commitment with no-commitment came from Bohemia as it bumped into Calvin: in Hammett's it came from never believing in any kind of permanence and a mind that rejected absolutes.)

Toys in the Attic, with a splendid cast, was a success. The money came at the right time, because for a year I had known that death was on Hammett's face and I had worried about how we could manage what I thought would be the long last days.

It had been my habit to set the alarm clock for every two hours of the night: I would stumble down the hall to sit with him for a few minutes because he could sleep so little as he panted to breathe. Now it was possible to have a nurse and I looked forward to a whole night's sleep. But it didn't work that way: I didn't like a stranger in his room, I didn't want the night's sleep.

In 1962 I began an adaptation of Bert Blechman's novel *How Much*. The play was called *My Mother*,

My Father and Me and, by the time I finished, was half Blechman, half me. I thought, I think now, that it is a funny play, but we did not produce it well and it was not well directed. More important, I found that I had made some of the same mistakes I had made with *Candide:* I changed the tone midway from farce to drama and that, for reasons I still do not understand, cannot be done in the theatre.

The play waited in Boston for the New York newspaper strike to end. Once again I sat bewildered in a hotel room, making changes I did not believe in, this time under the pressure of how much money was about to go down the drain.

The playwright is almost always held accountable for failure and that is almost always a just verdict. But this time I told myself that justice doesn't have much to do with writing and that I didn't want to feel that way again. For most people in the theatre whatever happens is worth it for the fun, the excitement, the possible rewards. It was once that way for me and maybe it will be again. But I don't think so.

Arthur W. A. Cowan

T HEODORE ROETHKE and I stood in the back of the auditorium until the poet Babette Deutsch finished reading. I am a noisy audience in a theatre, moving my body and feet without knowing it, cracking the knuckles of my hands, coughing. But I had been quiet that night because Ted had been tapdancing in the back aisle to music only he could hear and several people in the last row had objected.

When Babette finished, somebody whose name I do not remember came onstage and said things I wanted to hear but couldn't because Ted said, very loudly, "I have just made up a poem. It begins 'Isn't it thrilling.' Now you write the next line. Go on, write the next line." I smiled because that's usually safe with drunks, but it didn't work.

"You don't want to write a poem with me. I don't

think you want to write a poem at all. O.K. We'll write a play together, just the two of us. What you say to that?"

He said it again and poked me in the ribs. "Sure, Ted. A play," and hoped he wouldn't poke me again.

"You say sure, anything, sure, because no matter how much work *I* do on our play people will think *you* wrote it and I won't get any credit. So we'll sign an agreement to have one name for both of us. What name would you like?"

I said, "Let's go sit down. My feet hurt."

"Not until we find a name. I know, I know, I've got it. We'll sign it with the salmon. How about Irving K. Salmon? I like that, Irving K. Salmon, a good name."

All through dinner there had been talk of a salmon but I didn't know if he was talking about a particular salmon or all salmon because sometimes he talked about their spawning habits, sometimes he talked of one or two or eight fishing trips he had made, and once he told me about a nun he knew in Seattle who had caught a giant fish and given it to him.

Then another man came onstage, Roethke gave a whoop, pulled me by the hand and dragged me down the aisle. "Now stop talking about our play. That can wait. I want to hear Cal."

We started into aisles that were already filled, backed out, crossed a number of annoyed people in the front row, and by this time had the full attention of our side of the house. Robert Lowell had started to read in a rather low voice by the time we finally sat down and I wondered how he would make out if Ted kept on talking. But he didn't. He sat hunched forward, moving his lips to the poems, smiling, applauding occasionally at the end of a line. After a long silence he said in a new, piping, child's voice that carried through our section, "The kid's good." I am sure the kid was good but I hadn't been listening: I was tired after hours of being moved around New York, the pounding, often incoherent talk, the energy that had made us sprint into the zoo, running from monkey house to bird house, and then amble through lunch only to sprint again to visit a friend of Ted's who turned out to have moved from New York two years before.

When the Lowell reading was over, Ted made for backstage. He was ahead of me, forgetting me I think. But I decided not to follow him and walked slowly home, not expecting to see him again until the next time he came East.

In front of my house were Lowell, Ted, Babette, and three other people. Ted lifted me from the ground and said, "I told 'em you'd be right along after you had finished your secret pint."

To this day I do not know who two of the strangers were, but I came to know the third and he is the reason for my writing now about that night. I came to know his face as well as my own, but I have no memory of it that first time, nor did I then know his name.

I remember only that I found myself yawning into the face of a man sitting near me, yawned in another direction, and a few minutes later became conscious that the man had been staring at me for a long time, not with a flirting look, but as if he were trying to understand something.

He said, "Where do you keep your books?"

"Upstairs. There is a kind of library."

"Thank you," he said, "I am glad to know that." And then I was too tired to care that neither of us said anything else. A little while later everybody went home except Ted, who was weaving back and forth in a kind of shuffle, his lips forming words I couldn't hear.

I said, "Ted, I'm sleepy."

He said, "Ssh. I've got it. I've got it. The best poem written in our time. Now listen carefully: 'Isn't it thrilling there's another Trilling?' Got it? 'Isn't it thrilling there's another Trilling?' Got it? 'Isn't it thrilling there's another Trilling?' "

The second time he poked me in the ribs with his pleasure in creation I said, sure, the poem was fine, but why didn't he go home. He gave me a sad, hurt look, fell on me from his side of the couch and went to sleep immediately. I got from under his dangerous weight without waking him, but the next morning when I came down for breakfast he was gone. There was a note on the table: "I tell you it *is* thrilling, the Trilling. And just you remember about Irving K. Salmon."

I don't know how I came to mix up the salmon with the flowers, but four or five days later, Helen, a black woman who had worked for me for many years, suddenly appeared in the reading room of the Society Library. When something important had happened, or she was disturbed, she made military gestures. Now she hit me on the shoulder, made a sign meaning I should follow her, and while we walked the few blocks to our house she said, "Mary is down with it again. This time she got her good reasons."

Mary and her husband Ed had been the janitors of the house for the many years I owned it. They were Irish, feckless, kind, and often drunk, at which time they scattered into excitable pieces over nothing more than the mail being late or a light bulb wearing out.

"What's the matter this time?"

"I tell you this time she got her good reasons. A child's coffin. A child's coffin has come to the house."

"A child's coffin?"

"In a pine box. Dripping."

Indeed there was a pine box in the hall, it was the size of a small child, it was dripping, and most of the red lettering of the sender had been washed away. One could still read, "Mother Joa — " and numbers that still had two eights in them. Mary and Ed were too upset for me to know or care whether they had been drinking, but when I said, "It smells of fish," Mary shrieked, went out into the street and was followed by Ed, who took her arm and led her off, I guess, toward their favorite Lexington Avenue bar.

Helen went to get the handyman from the apartment house next door and when he pried off the lid there was a large salmon lying on what had been a bed of ice. The fish was turning, not enough to make us sick, but enough to make us carry it out to the street and close it up again.

In time, it turned out that Roethke had sent the salmon, and we exchanged a number of letters about it, although it was never clear about "Mother Joa — " A further mix-up came about because while we were opening the salmon box a large basket of flowers arrived, Helen put them on the floor, and somehow they got thrown out in the salmon excitement. I don't know why I thought Roethke had sent the flowers, but I thanked him, and long after I knew he had not sent them, he wrote that they came as a tribute because I liked his greenhouse poems.

A few weeks later another basket arrived. There were two enclosed cards: one from the lady florist who wanted to know if I had received a basket sent a few weeks before, and a second card on which was printed "Arthur W. A. Cowan, Esquire" and then a designation I have long forgotten that meant he had something to do with the State of Pennsylvania. I did not recognize the name Cowan, had never before known an Esquire, wondered when you were entitled to use it. Later that day I tried to phone the lady florist to find out about Esquire, but the phone was busy and I forgot about the whole thing until a third, even fancier arrangement arrived, with the same card and a scribbled sentence that thanked me for a nice evening.

I don't know when or how I connected the name with the man who had asked me about the books. It may have been because Lowell told me that he had never met Cowan before the night of the poetry reading but that he knew his name because Cowan had been a large financial contributor to *Poetry*. Nor do I have any memory of how Cowan and I first came to have dinner together, and then to have another, and then to find ourselves good friends.

It is hard, indeed, to construct any history of Arthur, in part because he traveled so much, but mostly because he talked of his own past and present in so disjointed a fashion, often taking for granted that you knew what you could not have known, certain that you were pretending ignorance only to annoy him. He is the only person I have ever known who had no sense of time: he did not know whether he had met people last week or many years before, and once he told me he had been divorced for three years when, in fact, he had been divorced for fourteen. And so, in the first few months I knew him, I could follow very little of the mishmash of what he said, and knew only that he had gone to Harvard Law School, moved on to the Philippines, been poor and grown rich, now practiced law in Philadelphia, had a large number of brothers and sisters, three houses, and expensive motor cars which he was constantly exchanging to buy others.

His no sense of time was tied up with no sense of

place, yours or his, so that he was bewildered and angered if you didn't know the names of his friends or the kind of work he did, even though nothing had ever been said about them. For example, the third time we had dinner he told me that he had spent much of his childhood in a Philadelphia orphan asylum.

I said, "But you're not an orphan. You just spoke of seeing your mother yesterday."

He was at that minute, as at so many other minutes, complaining about the steak he was eating, joking with the waiter about taking it back.

The good humor turned immediately to anger. "God damn it. That's the silliest stuff I ever heard anybody talk. You don't have to be an orphan to get into an orphan asylum. We were poor. We didn't have enough to eat. So they put two of us in the joint. Then sometimes when my father got a job they'd come and get us for a while and then bring us back again. I've told you all that a hundred times before."

In those early days of knowing him, I still believed in reasonability and so I tried to say he could not have told me a hundred times before, we had only known each other a few months. But before I could say that, he was telling the waiter that the steak was fine, but his dinner companion wasn't. I would have been angry, as I was to be many such times in the future, but that night I put down his sharpness with me to painful memories of the orphanage years.

I said, "I'm sorry. It must have been a bad time for you."

"What the hell are you talking about?" he said for the next four tables. "It was the best God-damned time of my life. It was clean, and there was meat every day. They had books and it was there I learned to read. It was the best part of my life and you're an ass. Even you. All women. Every God-damned woman is an ass."

He shouted for the check, left the waiter an enormous tip, put me in a taxi and marched off. The next day almost the same arrangement of flowers arrived and I threw them out.

A few weeks went by, perhaps a month, and then I had a telephone call. He said, very cheerfully, "What's the weather like?"

"It's a sunny day, but not for you and me. How is it in Philadelphia?"

"I'm in London and I called to say that I don't bear any grudge against you. I'll be back tomorrow and will take you to dinner."

I said I didn't intend to eat dinner the next night and he laughed and hung up.

The following night I was having a tray in bed and listening to the phonograph when Helen came in, turned off the phonograph and said, "Can you hear it now?"

"Hear what?"

"There's something bad going on in the elevator."

The house had a small self-service elevator, but once inside you needed a key to get out or somebody to open the door on our side. It was an old elevator, and although nothing much had ever happened to it, we were always conscious that it might stick or fall, or that, without care, we could admit intruders. I got out of bed, went to the elevator door, and when I asked who was there the rhythmic pounding ceased.

A voice said, "Who wants to know?"

"I want to know."

"Who are you?" a second, high voice said.

Helen said, "Tell them to go out the way they came."

The first voice said, "Who said that? How many thieves are in my house?"

The elevator began to move upward. Helen whispered, "Don't open the door. There's more than one." The elevator went past us and continued up to the floor of my tenant.

The high voice said, "Open up or I'll shoot the place down."

My tenants, above me, had an elderly Japanese cook, and after a minute we could hear him running down the service stairs.

Helen said, "There goes the Jap. You can't blame the poor soul."

Like most people my age, I had a hard time believing in city crime, perhaps in any kind of danger. So I said to Helen, as I would not say today, "Let the Jap in our service door and tell him there's nothing to be afraid of."

Then, very loudly, I shouted into the elevator door, "Please leave the house immediately."

"What'll you do if we don't?"

"Call the police. So go immediately."

"I've got a better idea," said a voice, now undisguised. "Get dressed and I'll buy you a decent steak."

A few hours later, sitting next to him in his newest Aston-Martin, having just had a bad steak in a restaurant somebody had told him about — somebody was always telling him about a restaurant; in the years I knew him I don't think we ever went twice to the same place — I said, "Arthur, you're too young for me."

"Without question. How old are you?"

"Forty-eight. Too old for your high-jinks. How old are you?"

He said he was forty-two, and I didn't know that night why he coughed so much after he said it, nor why he stared at me so hard when we reached my door.

I was to find out a few weeks later. It started when the mail brought an engraved invitation for a dinner party to be given in Philadelphia by Arthur W. A. Cowan, Esquire, in honor of Miss Lillian Hellman. Although the engraving proved that the party must have been planned weeks before, I had had on the Sunday before the arrival of the card a most disturbing time with Arthur.

On that bad Sunday, driving to the country on the first, lovely spring day, as the Saw Mill River Parkway went by the turnoff, I said that the farm I had owned for so many years was just around the bend, over the bridge. This was the first time since I had sold it that I found myself so close to it, and if I was silent for a long time it was because I was trying not to cry. After a while, he stared at me and asked irritably why, if I liked the place so much, I had sold it. He knew why, because I had told him, and so I didn't answer until the question was repeated.

"The House Un-American Activities Committee. The Joe McCarthy period. I went broke. I've told you all that, Arthur."

"Yeah," he said, "but I never understood it."

"O.K."

But he was not a man to leave things alone when the toothache of blind contention was upon him and so, after a while, he said again that he didn't understand what Joe McCarthy had to do with the sale of a farm and he thought I was just blaming my mistake on somebody else. I knew, of course, before that day that his politics were eccentric, going in one direction on some days, in another the next. He was solidly conservative, sympathetic to every piece of legislation that benefited the rich, was the attorney for millionaires like Del Webb, and yet was a close friend of Mark De Wolfe Howe of Harvard and the Philadelphia liberal lawyer Thomas McBride. We had had no previous political arguments, in part because the mishmash he talked was too hard to follow, but mostly because I had already learned that I could not, did not wish to explain, or be wise about, or handle the bitter storm that the McCarthy period caused, causes, in me, and knew even then that the reason for the storm was not due to McCarthy, McCarran, Nixon and all the rest, but was a kind of tribal turn against friends, half-friends, or people I didn't know but had previously respected. Some of them, called before the investigating committees, had sprinted to demean themselves, apologizing for sins they never committed, making vivid and lively for the committees and the press what had never existed; others, almost all American intellectuals, had stood watching that game, giving no aid to the weak or the troubled, resting on their own fancy reasons. Years later, in the 1960's, when another generation didn't like them for it, they claimed they had always been anti-McCarthy when they meant only they were sorry he was not a gentleman, had made a fool of himself, and thus betrayed them. That was, that is, to me the importance of the period — the McCarthys came, will come again, and will be forgotten — and the only time I ever heard all that properly analyzed was by Richard Crossman in London, and although I have never seen Mr. Crossman again, I have often wished that he had written it down. It is eccentric, I suppose, not to care much about the persecutors and to care so much about those who allowed the persecution, but it was as if I had been deprived of a child's belief in tribal safety. I was never again to believe in it and resent to this day that it has been taken from me. I had only one way out, and that I took: to shut up about the whole period.

And so on that day, driving in the country, I had

no words. But by the time we returned to New York I was so shocked at the insensibility that forced Arthur to make fun of what had harmed me and had sent Hammett to jail, that I felt nothing more than weariness and that I must not ever listen to such stuff again.

A few days later, I wrote Arthur a note saying that, found the note incoherent, tore it up, telephoned to say that I couldn't come to my party. The operator said he was in Paris. I telephoned him in Paris, the hotel said he was in London. I got him in London, and before I was able to say much of anything he told me that he had just taken a woman to dinner who had on a red coat, he hated red coats, would never see the woman again, didn't know what I was talking about but was in the middle of a meeting and had just bought me a bracelet. He hung up, and when I called him the next day I heard him tell the operator that Mr. Cowan was not available.

Somewhere in the next few weeks, I had dinner with Mark and Molly Howe in Boston. I told them about Cowan's defense of McCarthy. Mark got up from the table and didn't come back for a while. Molly said of course they had heard the same kind of thing, and when Mark came back in the room he said, "Arthur is unbearable, unbearable." He was so disturbed that we ate our dinner almost in silence, only speaking when the Howe children came in and out of the room. Mark and Molly walked me back to my hotel and, as we stood in front of it, Mark's fine face was obviously getting ready for something difficult. He said "He is unbearable. He is unbearable. But it is only fair to tell you that his opinions often have nothing to do with his actions. I once told him about a Communist who had no money for legal defense. He paid the total bill and sent the wife a thousand dollars. I don't know his friend Tom McBride, but I am told he has another form of the same story." Molly said she thought maybe Arthur was just plain crazy, but I think both of them were saying they would understand if I wrote him off, but they hoped I wouldn't. I didn't.

*   *   *

Thinking about that night a few weeks ago, I wrote to Molly Howe, who has moved to Dublin since the death of Mark Howe. She does not refer to that night, perhaps she doesn't remember it. But she understood Arthur:

Dear Lillian: What can I say of Arthur? It's like roaming through a churchyard and picking out the names of old friends on the tombstones. Mark, Johnny Ames, Arthur Cowan, Bunny Lang, my old father-in-law, Felix Frankfurter, McBride, Joe Wall, all of them strung together by one name — Arthur's.

Arthur becomes a game of true or false. What did you or I *really* know about him?

I first met him a few years after the war. We had dinner, Mark, Johnny Ames and I at the Athens Olympia. He was then triumphing over the winning of some case in New Jersey, I think, and I think it was connected with aspirin, which indeed one was inclined to need after a few hours in his rather fevered company.

And after that . . . flying visits into the law school. Everyone knocked out of their legal torpor. Griswold actually took to hiding. Always with a new sports car, wearing frightfully expensive rather gaudy clothes, driving like a madman; off to the Ritz; bursting into the Poets Theatre. You almost knew by the weather when Arthur was coming. Something threatening about those clouds massing in the north. And you never knew he was coming until he was there. And the letters from Paris, from London, from Rome, from Hawaii, from the desk of Arthur Cowan. It must have been a flying desk.

I've never had such a curious relationship with a man before or since. It was purely friendly, almost fraternal. I really confided in him. I wrote him constantly, and the things he told me as well — true or false? To this day I do not know which. Brought up in an orphanage, number 58. That's why the number of our house 58 Highland Street was so important. He was convinced he would die when he was 58! Father killed himself during the Depression. Worked his way through college by professional boxing. Belonged to a delightful club in New York called the Bucket of Blood. Was married once to some girl in Philadelphia who played too much tennis. It broke up. He had girls everywhere. Two of them in London, and he had great difficulty keeping them apart. A girl in Paris — very special. Never liked actresses. Never liked models.

All lesbians at heart and everywhere else. Once caught them in the very act.

Arthur as a houseguest was not good. Stayed with us four days on the Cape in 1954. Would only eat steak and lettuce three times a day. Insisted on going round three-quarters naked with shaven chest. This last revolted Mark. We had some stuffy neighbors to cocktails and Arthur sat in a stately manner (this was six P.M.) naked except for a slight pair of pants, reading a life of Byron. "Arthur," I hissed in passing, "this man is a brother-in-law of the Rockefellers." When I looked round again he had vanished, went upstairs, came down twenty minutes later in an immaculate white linen suit. Unfortunately the Rockefeller contingent had gone. The next night we all went to dinner in Provincetown with Isabella Gardner and her brother Bob. Sudden outbreak from Arthur, who had been curiously quiet all evening. Shouted at Bob Gardner, "You're stupid! Phony! Numb! Ridiculous!" All heads turned in his direction. Nobody could understand it. Belle G. was furious and would never meet him again. A year or two later during the summer he suddenly shouted at Perry Miller — we were having cocktails on the porch, Perry as I remember was offering some learned information on Cotton Mather — "You're posturing. Why are you always posturing?" I don't believe Arthur knew whether Cotton Mather was a textile or a boll weevil, but suddenly something infuriated him. As he was always in very good trim and looked, with that broken nose, like an aging but powerful boxer, nobody cared to take things up with him.

And his health. He was always having mysterious operations. He went through a period of having someone come in and give him an enema every day. He took royal jelly. Some great man in New York took care of his teeth. A splendid fellow in Switzerland for the eyes. Somebody in Philadelphia for the gallbladder and he told Mark he had himself sterilized in Paris. He didn't want any trouble of that kind. Paternity suits. Can't be too careful. And the diets. I never knew anyone go through such rigorous and varied diets. Do you remember the time he had to have raw parsley and carrots? Then there was the tablespoon of vinegar and all red meat phase and the exercises.

Every time he arrived there was a new and expensive camera. Color Polaroid long before anyone else and the constant taking of photographs was a ritual which had to be gone through on arrival and the camera was usually so new, so expensive, so complicated he didn't know how to use it. The cursing and swearing was heartrending.

Johnny Ames, for instance. Why did Arthur like such a New England Henry Jamesian old bachelor with very little money, of no importance in the world, because let's face it Arthur did like the Big Names. Why? And Johnny was fascinated by Arthur. They always had to meet when Arthur was in Cambridge. And they always talked about money. Do you remember Arthur talking about money? He talked about it the way some people talk about poetry. The voice was low and reverent, the face radiated a beautiful joy, and Johnny listened as if Arthur was the oracle, and Arthur advised Johnny on how to invest his little bit of capital. Advised him so well that by the time Johnny died he had almost doubled it. They conversed a great deal in French which was another bond and Johnny made the best martinis in Boston.

Why did he like V. R. Lang? A way-out blonde girl who wrote two good plays and some poetry and died of cancer aged thirty — a year after her very happy marriage. He met Bunny at the Poets Theatre, was fascinated by her play and fascinated by her world of Frank O'Hara, Bob Bly, Ted Gorey. It was through Bunny, in some way, he met you, Lillian, and moved into the Big World of Brains and never was happier. It all culminated for me at that wonderful house party, Birthday Party, weekend in Vineyard Haven that you gave for Arthur. How old was he then? It must have been twelve years ago. McBride was there and the Bernsteins and the Warburgs for dinner. Before Mark and I left that Monday morning, Arthur said to me, in that curious falsetto whisper: "It's not often you spend a weekend with all the people you like best. I have a feeling it only happens once." I have often thought of that since. Was it prescience?

He *was* a good friend. When Mark had a bad go of flu from overwork I told Arthur that Mark simply could not go on with the second volume of the Holmes and carry on a full teaching schedule at the law school. It took Arthur only a few weeks to manage that. Mark was relieved of half the law school load and Arthur paid the half of his salary on a grant basis. In fact, if it hadn't been for Arthur, vol. II would never have been written, and if it hadn't been for vol. II, Mark might have lived longer.

Then there was the episode of Little Hel. Do you remember our youngest daughter was always known by Arthur as Little Hel? One afternoon he and Mark went for a walk round Eagle Pond on the Cape and unknown to them Little Hel took it into her head to follow them through bush and through briar a good mile on her own wobbly legs. She caught up with them eventually and Arthur couldn't get over it. The courage! The guts! The determination! He carried her back the rest of the way on his shoulders. He was almost crying. Of course he was going to mention her in his will. That well-known will of Arthur's that you and so many others were going to benefit by.

Did you ever read his poems? He brought out a book of poems I think in the late Forties. I had a copy once. God knows where it went. They were, of course, very bad.

And then those books inscribed to us by authors who had never heard of us, with Arthur standing over them with a gun. "To my dear friends Mark and Mollie Howe from André Maurois, with the compliments of Arthur Cowan." *You* must have several shelves of them.

He was a James Bond character. You remember

the sudden sinking of the voice to a whisper and the shifty look around and quick glance over the shoulder? What *was* he up to?

Well, he died alone on a dusty road in Spain, our friend, and we don't even know the truth about that.

*   *   *

And so I went to the party. I was taken first to what he called the guesthouse — Cowan owned two houses in Philadelphia — and then hustled around to where he lived in the few weeks of the year when he lived in any one place. It was a handsome old house in Rittenhouse Square, the windows spoiled with ugly draperies, the furniture heavy expensive copies of what the movies think is an English greathouse library. I dislike dark rooms and so, without plan, I went to one of the windows and pushed aside the draperies to see the view. Arthur dashed for the draperies, closed them and shrieked at me: "My books! My books! Don't do that."

"Don't do what?"

"Don't let in any light. It will harm the bindings. Why don't you know such things? I'll tell you why — because you don't have a fine binding in the world."

"I don't like them," I said. "If I had the courage, I'd throw out all my books, buy nothing but paperbacks, replace them — "

"I can't stand what you're saying, I can't stand it. You're not fit to touch a book in this house. I forbid you to *touch my books*."

The first guest came in on the shouting. Arthur im-

233

mediately put an arm around me, his voice low, immensely loving. "This, I am proud to say, is my friend Lillian Hellman."

It was the usual cocktail stuff before dinner, but I was uneasy at being shown off and uncomfortable under the almost constant stare of a pretty girl across the room. At dinner I sat next to Tom McBride, whom I liked immediately. I knew that he had defended two radicals during the McCarthy period, and when I spoke of it and said there weren't many lawyers, certainly not successful ones, who had such courage, McBride pointed down the table to Cowan.

"That nut made it possible. I couldn't afford to take the cases, with a family and growing children, couldn't have involved my law partners. Cowan gave me all I needed through that time even though he hated what I was doing. He's a nut, but you'll get used to him, if you can stay with the nuttiness without wearing out. God knows what goes on in his head, if anything, but he'll kick through every time, without questions, and without wanting thanks, for the few people he has any respect for, and you're already one of them, the only woman it's ever happened with, and you must remember that."

I did remember it a few years later. Cowan said, "What's the matter with you? You haven't said a word for an hour." I said nothing was the matter, not wishing to hear his lecture about what was. After an hour of nagging, by the repetition of "Spit it out," "Spit it out," I told him about a German who had fought in the International Brigade in the Spanish Civil War, been badly wounded, and was now very ill in Paris without any money and that I had sent some, but not enough.

Arthur screamed, "Since when do you have enough money to send anybody a can to piss in? Hereafter, I handle all your money and you send nobody anything. And a man who fought in Spain has to be an ass Commie and should take his punishment."

I said, "Oh shut up, Arthur."

And he did, but that night as he paid the dinner check, he wrote out another check and handed it to me. It was for a thousand dollars.

I said, "What's this for?"

"Anybody you want."

I handed it back.

He said, "Oh, for Christ sake take it and tell yourself it's for putting up with me."

"Then it's not enough money."

He laughed. "I like you sometimes. Give it to the stinking German and don't say where it comes from because no man wants money from a stranger."

I sent the money to Gustav and a few months later had a letter from his wife asking if I knew anything about an American who had appeared at the hospital, left an envelope for Gustav with five hundred dollars, refused his name, spoke fine French, and had asked the nun at the desk if she fucked around very much.

But that day after the Philadelphia dinner party, the day he shoved in my pocket the largest and most vulgar topaz pin I have ever seen, and was strangely silent and thoughtful, was the day that marked our relationship for the rest of his life. We were driving back to New York — it is strange that almost every memory of Arthur is connected to a restaurant or to a car — and I had not talked to him very much because I sensed that he was on the verge of a temper. (I was to realize in the years to come that sadness often looked like temper, often turned into it, as if he were rejecting despair for something healthier.) As Arthur slowed down from his usual speed of a hundred miles an hour to avoid hitting two other cars, he said, "I'm the only good driver in America. Sons of bitches." Then he sighed. "Well, I might as well tell you, that's that. All my friends last night think you're too old for me."

I laughed. "Too old for what?"

"For me. They think that wouldn't be any good. I'm five or six years younger than you are." This was to be accepted throughout the years I knew him.

"What wouldn't be any good?"

He shifted around. He was uneasy, embarrassed, and that was always one step in front of irrationality. I should have been ready.

"You know what I'm talking about. Stop pretending."

"I don't know what you're talking about, Arthur."

"You know damn well. You're a combination of shyster lawyer and Jesuit. I mean you are too old for me to marry. That's what I mean and you made me say it."

I said, "That's not the way it is or ever could be."

"It's always the way it is. For every Goddamn broad that ever lived. Marriage, marriage, marriage."

"Not for me. Twice in my life, maybe, but not about you. I wouldn't marry you, Arthur, I never even thought about it."

"Like hell you wouldn't, like hell." He stopped the car in the middle of the Pennsylvania Turnpike. "You're lying. You'd marry me in a minute. Maybe not for anything but my money, but I'm not marrying you, see?"

I opened the door of the car and got out, getting home late that night by walking a long way to a place that suggested I call another place for a taxi.

But this time, the next day, in fact, I called him. I had not slept much that night, waking up to read, and to think about Arthur. I was what he wanted to want, did not want, could not ever want, and that must have put an end to an old dream about the kind of life that he would never have because he didn't really want it. We have all done that about somebody, or place, or work, and it's a sad day when you find out that it's not accident or time or fortune but just yourself that kept things from you. Years later, when Arthur was telling me about "a beautiful model who double-crossed me when I'd have given her the money without the double-cross," I told him what I had thought that night when he blamed my age and his friends for not wanting to marry me. He patted my arm and said, "Aah. Aah. Sometimes you're not an ass. Why don't I buy you a pound of caviar?"

But when I say years later and things like that, I

am not sure they are accurate. I did sometimes make notes in a diary, I have a large number of letters from Arthur, I remember more about him than I do about most people, and I know I can put together the order of his words with accuracy, but time, in his case, skips about for me, and I often mix up the places where we met, so that something that might have happened in Paris I have possibly transferred to Martha's Vineyard or Beverly Hills. The passing of time, the failure of memory, did not cause those confusions: they were always there. Perhaps because we never shared ordinary days together, more probably because everything about his life, the present and the past, was in jump-bites: he would tell a story about friends but he would start the story in the middle; he would ask you to regret a building he had just sold when he had not told you he had ever owned it; if he told a joke he would start with the last line and go backward; if he wanted to talk about a woman he was tired of, he started to tell you about another woman he had been tired of twenty years before.

I did piece together a kind of history, but I am not sure how much of it happened before I met him or after I knew him, since there was no way of sorting the past from the present. I knew that he didn't practice law much anymore, but that he himself was always suing somebody or some organization, and since that happened at least four or five times a year, I would get the details and the results mixed up. I knew that he had made a lot of money, before I met him, as counsel for a large drug company in a patent suit

and that he took stock instead of a legal fee. (It is in-
dicative that Molly Howe remembers the legal fight as
having to do with aspirin and I remember it as ben-
zedrine, and it was probably neither.) I knew that he
was a large investor in the stock market and a brilliant one. But I only knew that because sometime in
the first two years I knew him, he said, "Where is
your money invested?"

"I don't have much anymore. I have the house on
82nd Street, but — "

"What the hell did you do with all you earned?"

I said we were on a sensitive subject, the Joe Mc-
Carthy period and no work in Hollywood and the In-
ternal Revenue Department's refusal to let Hammett
have a nickel of his royalties, and thought we better
not get into an argument.

He said, "Don't tell me the reasons. Just go upstairs and get me all your records. Checkbooks, mort-
gages, everything. You'll starve in the streets without
me, that's where you'll end."

The following day I telephoned to say I needed my
checkbook because I forgot I was leaving in a few
days for London. Arthur said, "I'll give it to you in
the airport." Of course I thought he meant the airport
in New York and tried to reach him when he wasn't
there. He was waiting for me in the London airport
and swore that he had told me that. He had a new
Rolls-Royce, his third in about two years, and drove
me to the hotel. As I was signing, and the manager
came to greet me, Arthur said, "One room, not two,
and make it a cheap one. Miss Hellman has wasted

more money than anybody since Hubert Delahantey."

It was many references later, and many years, before I asked about Hubert Delahantey. It turned out he never existed in life: he was a rich American drunk who threw away all his money and died in a Paris garret in a novel Arthur had once bought at a French railroad bookstand but whose title he couldn't remember.

The following night, when the *Candide* rehearsals were over, Arthur came around to the theatre to take me to a new restaurant somebody had just told him about. After he had gone through his usual denunciation of the steak, he put my checkbook on the table.

"From now on you can have fifty percent of what you earn. I will invest the rest. You know nothing about money and are a disgrace. You'll end in a charity hospital and die without a pot to piss in or a bone to chew."

I said, "You talk too much about my death. And if that's the way it's going to be then I won't die much different from the rest of the world."

"You're the kind of fool who has forgotten more than you ever learned," he said so loudly that the next table of six upper-class English ladies and gentlemen looked down at their plates.

I said, "The English don't raise their voices, Arthur, although they may have other vulgarities."

"Fuck the British. I think they were in collusion with the Germans all through the war."

At the next table one man spoke to another man and the second man got up and came to our table. Arthur rose, grinning with pleasure.

He said, "My dear, good sir. During my attendance at Harvard, a university situated in Boston, the Athens of America, I was middleweight intercollegiate boxing champion and I am flattered that you recognize me. Let me buy you a drink."

The man, who was a tall, good-looking example of Empire, said he did not wish a drink, but he felt impelled to say that he thought insults to the English in their homeland were totally inappropriate for a foreign guest. Arthur gave a mirthless bad-actor laugh and said he wasn't anybody's guest; his hotel and this restaurant were gyp joints, what the hell did guest mean when you paid your way and the billions we spent with the Marshall Plan?

I got up and said, "I'm going to the toilet. Leave a note what jail you're in or what hospital."

When I came back Arthur had joined the English table and was sitting with his arm around the tall gentleman. After he had introduced me he whispered that Sir Francis was a distinguished barrister, they had many friends in common. After half an hour I said I was tired and wanted to go to bed.

Sir Francis said, "You're not going back to the toilet?"

I didn't much understand that or the giggles that went round the table until Arthur, walking me to the hotel, said, "They didn't like your saying toilet. I don't either and have always meant to tell you. Why can't you say ladies' room like other people? Sir Francis didn't like it for his wife. He said, 'I've heard of Hellman. But even an actress needn't say toilet.'"

"And what did you say, Arthur?"

"I said Miss Hellman is a playwright, most distinguished, and they made me name the plays. Anyway, we're invited to dine in the country with them tomorrow. Don't wear that tweed coat. Wear something quiet, black."

When we got to the hotel I said, "I am now going upstairs to the toilet and so I won't be able to go to the country with you tomorrow. If you don't tell them you are a Jew they'll think you're charming, but you can even tell them that if you also tell them how rich you are and very possibly good business for them."

We did not mention Sir Francis again until many months after we had both returned to New York and after somebody told me that Arthur had appointed him his representative in London.

I said, "Nice about you and Sir Francis. Have you given him enough business to install a toilet?"

"So you've heard about her," he said. "Want to see her picture?"

He took out of his wallet one of the many snapshots he was always taking with the most expensive of cameras he had just broken. A youngish woman was standing against a very large house, her entire body and face shaded by giant trees.

242

"Admit that she's a beauty," Arthur said.

"I can't see her. You can never see anybody in your pictures."

"I should tell you that I may decide to marry her."

"Who is she?"

"She is the niece of Sir Francis. A great beauty. I call her Lady Sarah."

(He did not lie, I guess. He did call her Lady Sarah but it was only last year that I discovered her name was not Sarah, she had no title, and neither, for that matter, did Sir Francis. Arthur had bestowed the titles upon them as a sign of the esteem he then felt.)

It is a strange side of many women that they are jealous even when they do not want the man, but I was old enough to watch for that and wait it out. I suppose I waited it out without speaking because after a while he said, "Don't worry."

I said I wouldn't and he said he thought I should and I asked him why and he said I was hiding things and he didn't like me when I did that. After we had batted that around for a long time, he said, "Don't you, don't you, well?"

"Don't I what?"

It is hard now to believe that I didn't know what he wanted me to feel and say and certainly the stumbling words, so unlike him, the sadness in the face, should have told me. But even if I had known in time I am not sure I could have said it.

"Don't I what?"

The sadness disappeared. He clipped out the words, "Worry about my money. You don't have to. Marry or not I'll take care of you."

I said I was having more trouble than usual finding out what he was talking about, and when he shouted, "My will. After I die. That's what I'm talking about," I thought it wiser to be off in another direction. So I asked him what had happened to the lady in Philadelphia and the one in Paris, had he told them about Lady Sarah?

"I'm through with them. If you ever listened you'd have known that months ago. Tomorrow morning I am flying to Hollywood for a vasectomy. Between that shit orthodontist and the abortions I spent fifteen thousand six hundred dollars last year."

The complaints about the orthodontist were old stuff but the vasectomy was new. I said, "If you're getting married why do you want a vasectomy?"

"Who wants children in this stinking world? I spent my life wondering why they ever had me. Who wants to throw out five thousand six hundred dollars on abortions?"

"You," I said, "for ladies who pocket four thousand of it."

We were at my front door. I said, "Arthur, you know that Hammett lives here now, is very sick, that means I don't get much sleep and am tired most of the time. Good night."

"So you don't want to talk about my marriage? If it worried you, you were going to miss me, that would be something else. But you're just afraid the marriage will cut you out of my will, no money for you. I've told you, and I'll keep my word, I'll take care of you."

And he pushed me through my door and went down the street. I stood in the kind of anger I hadn't known for many years but which, even as a young child, I knew was uncaring of consequence, without control, murderous. I ran down the street and caught him as he was stepping into a taxi. I grabbed his arm and spun him around and spoke in the tones of quiet reasonability which have always been for me the marks of greatest anger. "Stop trying to buy me. You've been doing it too long. Not you or my mother's family or anybody else and just maybe because I am frightened it could happen. So skip me and have your vasectomy and your teeth fixed and your face operated on again and leave me alone and don't mention money or your Goddamn will again."

I stopped in pain at what I had let slip. For two years I had pretended that I didn't know that this interesting-looking man didn't like his face, had had two operations in Hollywood to correct what he didn't like, and neither had corrected anything except to make him look assembled and had taken away the lively brightness, the amusing crinkles of time, all that had been good.

He said quietly, "You don't think the operations made me look better?" Then he turned and took a long time to pay off the taxi driver and when I saw

his face the tears in his eyes had stopped. He took
my arm and we walked up and down the same Madison Avenue block for an hour or so, neither of us
speaking. Then, from the corner, I saw the light in
Hammett's room go on, which meant that the night
was over for him. We turned down to the house.

I said, "There would be no meaning to any apol-
ogy, no sense saying I didn't mean to hurt you because I did. When I get like this it's better to be rid
of me." We shook hands and I went upstairs.

One likes to think that words are understood, that
what has been painful or forbidden will not happen
again. But a few weeks later I had a note from Arthur: "I canceled the vasectomy, although I'll probably have it another time. If then I die on the operating table, you'll be a very rich woman."

I can no longer remember how long after that night
we let each other rest in a kind of unplanned mora-
torium, but long after his death, one of his many
stockbrokers told me that during that time the market
had fallen sharply and that Arthur had put up a good
deal of his own money to carry the margin account he
had insisted I have; and sometime during that period
a puzzling letter arrived from Barclays Bank in London telling me that Mr. Arthur W. A. Cowan had in-
structed them to notify me that in the event of his
death securities had been placed in their vaults for
me, although, of course, they could not reveal the nature or the amount. It was with that letter that I knew
he had understood nothing of what we had said on our

long walk up and down Madison Avenue and that there would never again be any point in telling him that what was proof of friendship to him wasn't, necessarily, for me. I felt self-righteous about that, as I frequently have about other people's money stuff, until Helen, a few days after Christmas, showed me a hundred-dollar bill Arthur had sent her.

"My," she said.

"If you want to send it back, don't worry about me."

"He means no harm," she said. "You never understood that."

Helen was a fine cook, the best I've ever known, and the nicest times wo had together were in the kitchen. It had long been our habit, if we were alone, to make each other a gift dinner: she cooked me something I liked and I made her something she had come to like, my "foreign stuff," which she pretended she could never learn. That night I was making her saffron rice.

"Buy yourself a new coat with the hundred. You need it."

"No, I don't. The hundred dollars came pinned to a new coat. It's too small, of course."

Helen was a very big woman and the picture of Arthur trying to guess her size made me laugh.

"The coat be good for my niece. He means well. Men are different. You ain't ever learned that."

"Better than we are, worse?"

"Different. Where is Mr. Cowan?"

I thought I knew what she meant. She could barely

write the alphabet and could spell very few words. "You can thank him on the phone."

"I ain't worried about thanks and neither is he. *You* ought to write him, it's a shame. He's doing what we all must do, come soon, come late, getting ready for the summons, and you ought to put out a hand."

That kind of talk was a part of her Catholic convert nature: it had happened before. If I argued with her there was a chance of depriving her of what she needed, but to be silent made hypocrisy between us and she had often played at seeing which she could catch me at. But now, although I only half understood, I was disturbed.

"Getting ready for the summons? What do you mean?"

When she didn't answer me, I said, "You talk too much about death. And he's a Jew. We don't get ready for the summons."

"Jew, not Jew. Nobody's anything. We all lost sheep."

I had heard this many times before and I knew I could annoy her by quoting the Reverend Whittier, a famous Negro backwoods preacher of her childhood and my mother's. "Sheep? The Reverend Whittier didn't like sheep. He said, 'Rise up and make yourself in the image of the lion. Throw off the shackles, grab away the whip, cut the chains of your oppressors as the lion would spring from — ' "

"Oh, sure," she said, "sure enough. If we took away

the whip and cut the chains the white man would atom us out."

I laughed because I knew she wouldn't like it. She said, "I ain't talking about black nor white. I'm talking Bible, the summons to the Lord. The horn's over the hill and Mr. Cowan's been hearing it for years."

"Mr. Cowan's been hearing nothing but the sizzling of steaks, the crackle of money and airplane engines. What are you talking about?"

"Write him," she said. "Tell him my coat's fine and the money too."

All my life, beginning at birth, I have taken orders from black women, wanting them and resenting them, being superstitious the few times I disobeyed. So I did write about the money and the coat and for months received no answer. But in June of that year, a few months after Helen, Hammett and I moved to Martha's Vineyard, I had a note from him saying he'd like to come up for my birthday. I postponed telling Dash that he was coming. He had never met Arthur but he didn't like visitors, didn't like their seeing how sick he was, and would disappear into his part of the house during any visit. In any case, I didn't expect Cowan until the 20th, and so on the 17th of June, returning from market with a good many packages, I was surprised and nervous when I saw a Rolls-Royce parked in the drive.

Dash was sitting in the living room. Before I spoke he put up a warning hand and pointed outside to the terrace. The local chief of police was there watching a figure in the distance running up and down the beach.

"What's happened? Cowan was coming in a few days. I forget to tell you — "

Dash said, "He came in here all done up in a motorcycle helmet, carrying a gun. He pointed the gun at me and said, 'Put 'em up, sir, and hand over the jewelry.' It didn't worry me because I know a toy gun when I see it, but it worries the police because he did the same thing at the gas station, where they don't know a toy gun."

Dash was a good-natured man, but in the last, bad, suffering years almost anything was too much for him.

I said, "Sorry. What should I do?"

"Cowan is down on the beach doing push-ups or something. Go upstairs and bring down the toy gun."

When I came back with it — it had been sitting on top of the collected works of Yeats — Hammett went out to the terrace and from the window I could see him and the police chief looking at the gun and speaking words I couldn't hear. The policeman took the gun, waved at me through the window, and climbed the steps to his car.

Hammett went to his end of the house and I followed him up the stairs, bracing myself against the fall I always thought he would have. He put himself on the bed and stared at me as he always did when the years had done nothing to convince him that he knew much about me.

I said, "I didn't know he was coming today."

He closed his eyes. I said, "Is something the matter? Can I get you something?"

"No. I'm just thinking that for the first time in my life I've met a crazy man who is pretending that he is crazy and wondering why you never see danger. Maybe it's what saves you. Let me know when he leaves."

Arthur stayed for three days. He never asked about Hammett, Hammett never asked about him. On the last day of the visit, we took a picnic lunch to an ocean beach. After he had done his push-ups, taken his mile run, we had a nice day, full of disconnected talk about people and places, an occasional passing reference to Lady Sarah. On the ride home Arthur fished out a folded check from the glove compartment. It was made out to me for ten thousand dollars.

"What's this about?"

"It's not a birthday present. You earned it. Remember the Soloway case, the lawsuit I told you about? You said maybe I should just tell the truth because I'd get anything else mixed up."

He laughed with pleasure at the memory and I tried to remember which of the many lawsuits was called Soloway. "Well, only a first-rate shyster mind like yours could have thought that up. I won the case and that's your part. You'll need it when I die."

"Are you going to die again?"

"You're not to ask questions because they've forbidden me to answer."

"They?"

"Yes, this time, *they*. I have taken an important job with the government and an oath not to reveal what it's about. I am telling you that much because my travels may seem odd to you from now on."

"Odder than usual?"

"Odder than usual. That's why I want you to have the check. If I am killed, of course, there will be more for you, the securities at Barclays Bank."

I waited until that night, always his choice for driving because he could reach higher speeds, and put his check in the glove compartment of his car. As he came up the steps with his bags and got into his car, I said, "I don't like CIA spy stuff anywhere, Arthur, and I am too old to waste time talking about how such people are needed, I guess, in every country. I don't ever want another fight with you, so this will be the last time — "

He said, quietly, "Mark Howe said the same thing a few days ago. He believed that I don't lie. Do you?"

"Yes."

"I don't work for the CIA. I never even heard about them until Mark explained. I don't like people who spy on other people, either. It's not the CIA I am working for and I swear to it. But I owe you and Mark the truth. My new bosses did question me about both of you. I said you were about as radical as rice and Mark was the most distinguished man at Harvard and if I had to listen to one word against either of you, then to hell with the whole thing. They're gentlemen, my new bosses, and they apologized."

I said I was glad they were gentlemen and then,

somehow touched, I said I didn't have to know what foolishness he was up to and I didn't want to part with him ever.

He said, "We're never going to part. I always knew that," and the car roared out of the driveway.

I telephoned Mark the next morning and asked him who he thought "they" were. He said he didn't know, couldn't believe the job was of any importance because he was going on the assumption that nobody with any sense would allow Arthur to make decisions, except in the field of law, and he wasn't even sure about that.

About a year later, on the opening night of Simone Signoret's production of *The Little Foxes* in Paris, I made the guess that the job had something to do with the Common Market, although there was never anything to prove that true. Arthur had ordered twenty tickets for the opening night and was sitting next to Jean Monnet, who in the few minutes I spoke to him after the play told me that he found Arthur "a brilliant financier" and so did "other countries." I was too sad about the evening to ask the questions that probably wouldn't have been answered anyway. I wanted only to get out of the Théâtre Sarah Bernhardt.

I had arrived for the last two weeks of rehearsals. Arthur met me at Orly Airport and we had a good evening. His love of Paris was always a pleasant thing to watch, but it was the last good evening I was to have until I left Paris the day after the opening of the play.

Much in the theatre always goes wrong, it's as if

from the beginning it was intended that way, but I had never before seen so much go bad so early: it was an awkward, too literal translation of the play; it was in a theatre meant for a pageant or an ice show; the set, which was intended only to show the middle-class indifference of a woman who had all her life been on her way to another house, was cluttered and decorated with the largest and most demanding objects I had ever seen on a stage; and the Texas sombreros chosen for Alabama bankers became a large and dangerous argument between Simone and me when, of course, they were only a small symbol of our irritation with each other.

Simone Signoret is an intelligent, charming woman, as remarkable in front of a camera as she is bewildered by a stage. Not knowing much makes many people in the theatre turn natural sense and humility into nonsense and pretense. It is understandable, it is sad, but it is also difficult and tiresome. And I am often no good with actors or directors. I do not speak when I should, speak out when I shouldn't; I praise in order to hide complaints and that is recognized; and my manners grow excessively good to hide anger that can't be hidden. I thus offend more than if I had had an open fight.

Every evening, after rehearsals, Arthur came to the theatre to take me to dinner, bewildered, he told me later, at a side of me he had never seen before. I would sit silent, unable to eat the good food, drinking too much of the wine, smiling at the wrong places in his complicated stories, shaking my head when I should have laughed. The night before the official opening his patience was coming to an end: why did I worry about an old play when he had made me enough money to live well for the next few years? Why did I make faces about his newest diet, buttermilk with melted butter and cheese? Did I want to see a picture of Lady Sarah in a sable coat he had bought her? Why was there a copy of Büchner on my bed table when I knew how he hated Germans? Had I read *Candy* in the French edition he had given me? I must say immediately what I thought of *Candy*. There was justice in his impatience, but the questions were provocative. I was tired and so, trying not to answer him, I wrote on the back of the menu, "Arthur is a man of unnecessary things. That's sad, but there's no cure. Did I make that up or have I read it?"

He said, "I've asked you three times. What do you think of *Candy?*"

"A nasty way to make a buck." And waited for the trouble.

I don't think he heard me because he said, "Roscoe Pound saved me. At the end of my first year in Harvard Law School I didn't have enough money to come back for the second. Pound called me in and said he'd find the money for me to get through. That was before I married the tennis player whose family had never read a book. They wouldn't have liked *Candy*, either. The ignorant bastards."

"O.K., Arthur, I see what's coming."

"I only started out to say I have been faithful to you in my fashion, Cynara, you and the Harvard Law School, and not much else."

(As I write these words I would not believe them, but I have a letter, written about a week later, in which they are repeated exactly as they came that night.)

"I get tired of other women."

"What's happened to Lady Sarah and the marriage?"

"So Pound got the law school to make me the loan and when he called me in to tell me I could stay, well, I can't tell you — Anyway, I cried so hard afterward that I hit a guy in the cafeteria who asked me why my eyes were red. When I die, I will take good care of my sister, I hate the rest of my family, but I'll leave her enough so she can support them, and then the rest is for the Harvard Law School and you."

I said, "Why don't you do things while you're alive and then not so many people would look forward to your death, which may be the longest in history?"

"O.K.," he said, "I'll buy you a house."

"I have a house."

"Then you'll have two houses. You're no problem, but what should I do for Harvard Law School?"

I started to say fuck the Harvard Law School, I've got other problems, but I said, without interest, "Maybe a scholarship as a thank you to Pound?"

He got to his feet, pulled me up, embraced me until I lost my breath. "Wonderful. When it comes to the clinches, you're not such an ass. That's just what I'll do. Now stop being so sad about *Foxes*, I promise you I am never going to marry Lady Sarah."

A few months later he told me something about the scholarship and I think he remembered to tell me because we were on our way to dine with Ben Kaplan, a member of the Harvard Law faculty. Arthur was in a gay, charming good humor that night — he liked lawyer academics, respected them — until a man sitting next to him spoke of Goethe. Then one of the storms that came across the ocean of his years broke with tornado force, more out of control than I had ever seen before, without sense or reason, from depths so unknown and frightening that even these strangers turned aside in pity or embarrassment. Arthur was shouting to a silent table that Goethe was an old German ass, like all Germans, past and present. Then a woman, maybe the bravest or the silliest, asked about Bach and Beethoven and I knew immediately that would make things worse because Arthur didn't like women to speak when he was angry, maybe because middle- and upper-class men had convinced him against his will that women shouldn't be shouted at or knocked to the floor. He suddenly grew dangerous quiet as he told her that nobody was sure Bach and Beethoven were Germans, and anyway they were musicians and what did that have to do with thinking? I was, as I had been many times before, torn with shame that he was my friend and a strong desire not to deny or desert him. So I made the wrong, nervous remark: I said it all came back to Arthur's never having forgiven the Germans for producing Karl Marx. The quiet tone was gone again: Arthur told the table that my ancestors were German, that I had, therefore, inherited the national villainies, that my grandmother's name was Marx and therefore I was related to Karl Marx, and was even numbskull enough to like Heine. Still mistakenly intent on diverting him — it sometimes could be done and then he was grateful for the extended hand — I said that I had always liked Heine's remark that when the Germans made a revolution they would first have to ask permission. Arthur shouted at me that even I should know that Heine meant the *Nazi* revolution because Heine was an early Nazi and he wouldn't any longer sit at a table with me or anybody else who had an ounce of German blood.

It was that night, at that table, as I watched him leave the Kaplan house and move down toward the beach, that I knew something had gone wrong with Arthur, now forever: the inside lines that hold most of us together had slackened or broken and bad trouble was ahead. The early deprivations, the lost belief that money solved the problems of his life, the wild traveling about, the women, perhaps even the mysterious new job, maybe all of it or only some, certainly much I didn't know about, had made the life into a line on a fishing reel that tangled and couldn't be untangled, held by a hand that didn't have the sense or the courage to cut the line and tie it together in another place. But I had to cut the line of me where it crossed and tangled with his, and that night I did it, although, I am glad to say, he never knew it happened.

I was not angry that night, I was never to be angry with him again. It was no longer possible to pay him the compliment of anger, and I think he knew it and was worried about it. We saw less of each other, but in that next year and a half I had more affectionate letters than ever before, and once he arrived late at night, directly off a European plane, with a charming gold pin, and once he told me he had used the securities in my name at Barclays Bank but not to worry because he had increased my inheritance in his will, and once he told me that I was his best friend and that he loved me, and a number of times we had pleasant evenings and he became, for the first time, almost a suitor, as if he was looking for the affection he felt he had lost. He had not lost it. The truth was more important to us both: he had become to me a man of unnecessary things and often I felt that he knew what he was, was gallant about the pain it caused him and tried to hide it from himself with new cars, new houses, new friends, new women half forgotten at the minute they were half loved, new faces for himself, teeth set and reset, even new writers, here and in France, subsidized too long for their always shabby talents, new banks, new stocks, a new city or village or ocean that

259

he liked so much one year and disliked so much the next.

The last time I ever saw him was an August week he came to stay with me in Martha's Vineyard. An old friend of mine was there, he liked her, and the three of us had a pleasant time. We raced to many beaches in his newest Rolls-Royce, the old having been bought a year before, we walked, we climbed cliffs where he would be waiting for me at the top to say that even if I was six years older than he I was still in bad shape, and he would prove that further by running down the cliff and for a mile stretch on the beach, the fine powerful body no heavier, he said, than when he had been young. And for once there were no boring lectures about new diets: he ate the delicious stuff that Helen cooked and kissed her after each meal.

I said to her, "Mr. Cowan looks fine, doesn't he?"

She stared at me and fished out of her pocket a piece of paper. It read, "Before I fly tonight to Paris, Air France, Flight 972, I wish to bequeath to Helen Anderson in case of my demise the sum of ten thousand dollars in repayment for her kindness during these years."

I laughed. "He does that often, with all the ladies he likes."

"It's not nice," she said.

A few hours later, Helen and I walked with him as he carried his luggage to the car. I said, "Have a good trip."

260

Behind me, Helen said, "It's not nice, this piece of paper about the money."

I said, "Oh, what difference does it make?"

He kissed us both, said something about coming to visit his new apartment in Torremolinos about which I had not previously heard, and started the engine. I don't think he heard Helen say, "Drive slow, Mr. Cowan. Pray the summons back."

On November 11, 1964, I came into a hotel in Mexico City to hear myself paged. The voice said that Cowan was dead, killed instantly when the Rolls-Royce was smashed in Seville. But the accident was not in Seville and he had not died instantly and he had not been driving the Rolls-Royce. No will was ever found, but Lady Sarah and the pretty lady from the Philadelphia party of so long ago came up with old letters, almost exactly like Helen's, and collected large sums of money. In time, I asked Helen if she didn't want to present her note for collection, the going was good, and for a while she pretended not to know what I was talking about. Then one day she told me she had torn up the note as we stood saying good-bye to him that last day at the car door. The conflicting details of the accident, why a will disappeared that he certainly wrote and rewrote through the years, the failure even to find out what job he had been doing for what agency, all are to this day unexplained. If his life was puzzling, he entrusted the memory of it to people who have kept it that way. He has disappeared. I do not believe he would have wanted it that way. And he was not six years younger than I, he was two years older, and there was a girl with him when he died. She was unharmed in the accident, she was nineteen years old, and she was German.

"Turtle"

I HAD awakened at five and decided to fish for a few hours. I rowed the dinghy out to the boat on that lovely foggy morning and then headed around my side of Martha's Vineyard into the heavy waters of West Chop. Up toward Lake Tashmoo I found the quiet rip where the flounders had been running, put out two lines, and made myself some coffee. I am always child-happy when I am alone in a boat, no other boat to be seen until the light breaks through. In an hour I had caught nine flounders and a couple of tautogs that Helen would like for chowder and decided to swim before going home to work. The boat had drifted out, down toward the heavy chop, but there was nothing new in this, and I was never careless: I tied my two-pound stone to a long rope, carried it down the boat ladder with me, and took it out

to where I would swim near it. I don't know how long
it took me to know that I wasn't swimming but was
moving with incredible swiftness, carried by a tide I
had never seen before. The boat had, of course,
moved with me, but the high offshore wind was carrying it out of the rip into deep water. There was no
decision to make: I could not swim to the boat, I
could not force myself against the heavy tide. I
have very little knowledge of the next period of time
except that I turned on my back and knew that panic
was not always as it has been described. For a time
I was rigid, my face washed with water; then I
wasn't rigid and I tried to see where the tide would
take me. But when I turned to raise my head, I went
down, and when I came up again I didn't care that
I couldn't see the shore, thinking that water had
been me, all my life, and this wasn't a bad way to
die if only I had sense enough to go quietly and not
make myself miserable with struggle. And then — I
do not know when — I bumped my head against the
pilings of the West Chop pier, threw my arms
around a post, and remembered all three of us, and
the conversation that took place four days after the
turtle died when I said to Hammett, "You understood each other. He was a survivor and so are you.
But what about me?"

He hadn't answered and so I repeated the question
that night. "I don't know," he said, "maybe you are,
maybe not. What good is my opinion?"

Holding to the piling, I was having a conversation

with a man who had been dead five years about a turtle who had been dead for twenty-six.

Even in those days, 1940, it was one of the last large places in that part of Westchester County. I had seen it on a Tuesday, bought it on Thursday with royalties from *The Little Foxes,* knowing and not caring that I didn't have enough money left to buy food for a week. It was called an estate, but the house was so disproportionately modest compared to the great formal nineteenth-century gardens that one was immediately interested in the family who had owned it for a hundred and twenty years but who had, according to the agent, disappeared. (This was not true: eight or nine years later a young man of about sixteen or seventeen came by and asked if he could see the house and picnic at the lake. He said he had been born in the house and he took with him a giant branch of the hawthorn tree he said his mother had planted to celebrate his birth.)

In the first weeks, I closed the two guesthouses, decided to forget about the boxwood and rare plants and bridle paths, and as soon as Hammett sold two short stories we painted the house, made a room for me to work in, and fixed up the barn. I wanted to use the land and would not listen to those who warned me against the caked, rock-filled soil. I hired Fred Herrmann, a young German farmer, because I had an immediate instinct that his nature was close to mine, and together, through the years, we drove ourselves to the

267

ends of weariness by work that began at six in the morning and ended at night. Many of our plans failed, but some of them worked fine: we raised and sold poodles, very fashionable then, until we had enough profit to buy chickens; I took the money I got from the movie script of *The Little Foxes* and bought cattle and three thousand plants of asparagus we bleached white and sold at great prices. We crossbred ducks that nobody liked but me, stocked the lake with bass and pickerel, raised good pigs and made good money with them and lost that money on pheasants; made some of it back with the first giant tomatoes, the sale of young lambs and rich unpasteurized milk. But all that was in the good years before the place had to be sold because Hammett went to jail in the McCarthy period and I was banned in Hollywood after I was called before the House Un-American Activities Committee. The time of doing what I liked was over in 1952.

I have a jungle of memories about those days: things learned and forgotten, or half remembered, which is worse than forgetting. It seems to me I once knew a lot about trees, birds, wildflowers, vegetables and some animals; about how to make butter and cheese and sausages; how to get the muddy taste out of large-mouth bass, how to make people sick with the weeds I would dig and boil up according to all those books that say you can. The elegant Gerald and Sara Murphy grew very ill on skunk cabbage I had disguised according to an eighteenth-century recipe.

But the day I remember best was in the first spring

I owned the place. The snow had gone on the bridle paths and, having finished with the morning's work at the barns, I took Salud, the large poodle, and four of his puppies on an early morning walk to the lake. As we reached the heavily wooded small hill opposite the lake, Salud stopped, wheeled sharply, ran into the woods, and then slowly backed down to the road. The puppies and I went past him to the lake and I whistled for him, sure that he had been attracted by a woodchuck. But when I looked back he was immobile on the road, as if he had taken a deep breath and had not let it out. I called to him but he did not move. I called again in a command tone that he had never before disobeyed. He made an obedient movement of his head and front legs, stared at me, and turned back. I had never seen a dog stand paralyzed and, as I went back toward him, I remembered old tales of snakes and the spell they cast. I stopped to pick up a heavy stick and a rock, frightened of seeing the snake. As I heard Salud make a strange bark, I threw the rock over his head and into the woods, yelling at him to follow me. As the rock hit the ground, there was a heavy movement straight in front of the dog. Sure now that it was a snake about to strike, I ran toward Salud, grabbed his collar, and stumbled with the weight of him. He pulled away from me and moved slowly toward the sound. As I picked myself up, I saw a large, possibly three-foot round shell move past him and go slowly toward the water. It was a large turtle.

Salud moved with caution behind the turtle and as

I stood, amazed at the picture of the dog and the slowly moving shell, the dog jumped in front of the turtle, threw out a paw, and the jaws of the turtle clamped down on the leg. Salud was silent, then he reared back and a howl of pain came from him that was like nothing I had ever heard before. I don't know how long it took me to act, but I came down hard with my stick on the turtle's tail, and he was gone into the water. Salud's leg was a mess but he was too big for me to carry, so I ran back to the house for Fred and together we carried him to a vet. A week later, he was well enough to limp for the rest of his life.

Hammett was in California for a few weeks and so I went alone almost every day to the lake in an attempt to see the turtle again, remembering that when I was a child in New Orleans I had gone each Saturday with my aunt to the French market to buy supplies for her boarding house. There had been two butchers in the market who had no thumbs, the thumbs having been taken off as they handled snapping turtles.

Hammett came back to the farm upset and angry to find his favorite dog was crippled. He said he had always known there were snappers in the lake, and snakes as well, but now he thought we ought to do something, and so he began his usual thorough research. The next few weeks brought books and government publications on how to trap turtles and strange packages began to arrive: large wire-mesh cages, meant for something else but stared at for days until Hammett decided how to alter them; giant fishhooks;

extra heavy, finely made rope; and a book on tying knots. We both read about the origin of snapping turtles, but it didn't seem to me the accounts said very much: a guess that they were the oldest living species that had remained unchanged, that their jaws were powerful and of great danger to an enemy, that they could do nothing if turned on their backs, and the explanation of why my turtle had come out of the woods — each spring the female laid eggs on land, sat on them each day, and took the chance that the hatched babies would find their way to water.

One day, a month later perhaps — there was never any hurrying Hammett when he had made up his mind to learn about something — we went to the lake carrying the wire cages, the giant fishhooks, fish heads and smelly pieces of meat that he had put in the sun a few days before. I grew bored, as I often did, with the slow precision which was part of Dash's doing anything, and walked along the banks of the lake as he tied the bait inside the traps, baited the hooks, and rowed out with them to find heavy overhanging branches to attach them to.

He had finished with one side of the lake, and had rowed himself beyond my view to the south side, when I decided on a swim. As I swam slowly toward the raft, I saw that one limb of a sassafras tree was swinging wildly over the water, some distance from me. Sitting on the raft, I watched it until I saw that the movement was caused by the guyline that held one of the hooks Hammett had tied to the branch. I shouted at Hammett that he had caught a turtle and he called back that couldn't be true so fast, and I called back that he was to come for me quick because I was frightened and not to argue.

As he came around the bend of the lake, he grinned at me.

"Drunk this early?"

I pointed to the swinging branch. He forgot about me and rowed over very fast. I saw him haul at the line, have trouble lifting it, stand up in the boat, haul again, and then slowly drop the line. He rowed back to the raft.

"It's a turtle all right. Get in. I need help."

I took the oars as he stood up to take the line from the tree. The line was so heavy that as he moved to attach it to the stern of the rowboat he toppled backward. I put an oar into the center of his back.

He stared at me, rubbing his back. "Remind me," he said and tied the line to the stern. Then he took the oars from me.

"Remind you of what?"

"Never to save me. I've been meaning to tell you for a long time."

When we beached the boat, he detached the rope and began to pull the rope on land. A turtle, larger than the one I had seen with Salud, was hauled up and I jumped back as the head came shooting out. Dash leaned down, grabbed the tail, and threw the turtle on its back.

"The hook is in fine. It'll hold. Go back and get the car for me."

I said, "I don't like to leave you alone, you shouldn't be handling that thing — "

"Go on," he said. "A turtle isn't a woman. I'll be safe."

We took the turtle home tied to the back bumper, dragging it through the dirt of the mile to the house. Dash went to the toolhouse for an axe, came back with it and a long heavy stick. He turned the turtle on its stomach, handed me the stick, and said, "Stand far back, hold the stick out, and wait until he snaps at it."

I did that, the turtle did snap, and the axe came down. But Dash missed because the turtle, seeing his arm, quickly withdrew his head. We tried five or six times. It was a hot day and that's why I thought I was sweating and, anyway, I never was comfortable with Hammett when he was doing something that didn't work.

He said, "Try once more."

I put the stick out, the turtle didn't take it, then did, and as he did, I moved my hand down the stick thinking that I could hold it better. The turtle dropped the stick and made the fastest move I had ever seen for my hand. I jumped back and the stick bruised my leg. Hammett put down the axe, took the stick from me, shook his head and said, "Go lie down."

I said I wasn't going to and he said I was to go somewhere and get out of his way. I said I wasn't going to do that either, that he was in a bad temper with me only because he couldn't kill the turtle with the axe.

"I am going to shoot it. But that's not my reason

for bad temper. We've got some talking to do, you and I, it's been a long time."

"Talk now."

"No. I'm busy. I want you out of the way."

He took my arm, moved me to the kitchen steps, pushed me down and went into the house for a rifle. When he came out he put a piece of meat in front of the turtle's head and got behind it. We waited for a long time. Finally, the head did come out to stare at the meat and Hammett's gun went off. The shot was a beauty, just slightly behind the eyes. As I ran toward them the turtle's head convulsed in a forward movement, the feet carried the shell forward in a kind of heavy leap. I leaned down close and Hammett said, "Don't go too near. He isn't dead."

Then he picked up the axe and came down very hard on the neck, severing the head to the skin.

"That's odd" he said. "The shot didn't kill it, and yet it went through the brain. Very odd."

He grabbed the turtle by the tail and carried it up the long flight of steps to the kitchen. We found some newspapers and put the turtle on top of the coal stove that wasn't used much anymore except in the sausage-making season.

I said, "Now we'll have to learn about cutting it for soup."

Dash nodded. "O.K. But it's a long job. Let's wait until tomorrow."

I left a note under Helen's door — it was her day off and she had gone to New York — warning her there was a turtle sitting on the stove and not to be frightened. Then I telephoned my Aunt Jenny in New Orleans to get the recipe for the good soup of my childhood and she said I was to stay away from live turtles and go back to fine embroidery like a nice lady.

The next morning, coming down at six to help Fred milk the cows, I forgot about the turtle until I started down the kitchen steps and saw blood. Then, thinking it was the blood that we had spilled carrying the turtle into the house the evening before, I went on toward the barns. When I came back at eight, Helen asked me what I wanted for breakfast, she had made corn bread, and what had I meant by a turtle on the stove?

Going up to have a bath, I called back, "Just what I said. It's a turtle on the stove and you must know about snappers from your childhood."

After a few minutes she came upstairs to stare at me in the bathtub. "There ain't no turtle. But there's a mess of blood."

"On top of the coal stove," I said. "Just go have a look."

"I had a lot of looks. There ain't no turtle on top a stove in this house."

"Go wake Mr. Hammett," I said, "right away."

"I wouldn't like to do that," she said. "I don't like to wake men."

I went running down to the kitchen, and then fast back upstairs to Hammett's room, and shook him hard.

"Get up right away. The turtle's gone."

He turned over to stare at me. "You drink too much in the morning."

I said, *"The turtle's gone."*

He came down to the kitchen in a few minutes, stared at the stove, and turned to Helen. "Did you clean the floor?"

"Yes," she said, "it was all nasty. Look at the steps."

He stared at the steps that led to the cellar and out to the lawn. Then he moved slowly down the steps, following the path of blood spots, and out into the orchard. Near the orchard, planted many years before I owned the house, was a large rock garden, over half an acre of rare trees and plants, rising steep above the house entrance. Hammett turned toward it, following a path around the orchard. He said, "Once, when I worked for Pinkerton, I found a stolen ferris wheel for a traveling country fair. Then I lost the ferris wheel and, as far as I know, nobody ever found it again."

I said, "A turtle is not a ferris wheel. Somebody took the turtle."

"Who?"

"I don't know. Got a theory?"

"The turtle moved himself."

"I don't like what you're saying. He was dead last night. Stone dead."

"Look," he said.

He was pointing into the rock garden. Salud and three poodle puppies were sitting on a large rock, staring at something in a bush. We ran toward the garden. Hammett told the puppies to go away and parted the branches of the bush. The turtle sidling in an effort at movement, was trying to leave the bush, its head dangling from one piece of neck skin.

"My God," we both said at the same time and stood watching the turtle for the very long time it took to move a foot away from us. Then it stopped and its back legs stiffened. Salud, quiet until now, immediately leaped on it and his two puppies, yapping, leaped after him. Salud licked the blood from the head and the turtle moved his front legs. I grabbed Salud's collar and threw him too hard against a rock.

Hammett said, "The turtle can't bite him now. He's dead."

I said, "How do you know?" He picked up the turtle by the tail. "What are you going to do?"

"Take it back to the kitchen."

I said, "Let's take it to the lake. It's earned its life."

"It's dead. It's been dead since yesterday."

"No. Or maybe it was dead and now it isn't."

"The resurrection? You're a hard woman for an ex-Catholic," he said, moving off.

I was behind him as he came into the kitchen, threw the turtle on a marble slab. I heard Helen say, "My goodness, the good Lord help us all."

Hammett took down one of the butcher knives. He moved his lips as if rehearsing what he had read. Then he separated the leg meat from the shell, cutting

277

expertly around the joints. The other leg moved as the knife went in.

Helen went out of the kitchen and I said, "You know very well that I help with the butchering of the animals here and don't like talk about how distasteful killing is by people who are willing to eat what is killed for them. But this is different. This is something else. We shouldn't touch it. It has earned its life."

He put down the knife. "O.K. Whatever you want."

We both went into the living room and he picked up a book. After an hour I said, "Then how does one define life?"

He said, "Lilly, I'm too old for that stuff."

Toward afternoon I telephoned the New York Zoological Society of which I was a member. I had a hard time being transferred to somebody who knew about turtles. When I finished, the young voice said, "Yes, the *Chelydra serpentina*. A ferocious foe. Where did you meet it?"

"Meet it?"

"Encounter it."

"At a literary cocktail party by a lake."

He coughed. "On land or water? Particularly ferocious when encountered on land. Bites with such speed that the naked human eye often cannot follow the movement. The limbs are powerful and a narrow projection from each side connects them to the carapace — "

"Yes," I said. "You are reading from the same

278

book I read. I want to know how it managed to get down a staircase and up into a garden with its head hanging only by a piece of skin."

"An average snapper weighs between twenty and thirty pounds, but many have weighed twice that amount. The eggs are very interesting, hard of shell, often compared with ping-pong balls — "

"Please tell me what you think of, of, of its *life*."

After a while he said, "I don't understand."

"Is it, was it, alive when we found it in the garden? Is it alive now?"

"I don't know what you mean," he said.

"I'm asking about life. What is *life?*"

"I guess what comes before death. Please put its heart in a small amount of salted water and be kind enough to send us a note reporting how long the heart beats. Our records show ten hours."

"Then it isn't dead."

There was a pause. "In our sense."

"What is our sense?"

There was talk in the background noise and I heard him whisper to somebody. Then he said, "The snapping turtle is a very low, possibly the lowest, form of life."

I said, "*Is it alive or is it dead?* That's all I want to know, please."

There was more whispering. "You asked me for a scientific opinion, Miss Hellernan. I am not qualified to give you a theological one. Thank you for calling."

Ten or twelve years later, at the end of a dinner

party, a large lady crossed the room to sit beside me. She said she was engaged in doing a book on Madame de Staël, and when I had finished with the sounds I have for what I don't know about she said, "My brother used to be a zoologist. You once called him about a snapping turtle." I said to give him my regards and apologies and she said, "Oh, that's not necessary. He practices in Calcutta."

But the day of the phone call I went to tell Hammett about my conversation. He listened, smiled when I came to the theological part, went back to reading an old book called *The Animal Kingdom*. My notation in the front of this book, picked up again on a July afternoon in 1972, is what brought me to this memory of the turtle.

Toward dinnertime, Helen came into the room and said, "That turtle. I can't cook with it sitting around me."

I said to Hammett, "What will we do?"

"Make soup."

"The next time. The next turtle. Let's bury this one."

"*You* bury it."

"You're punishing me," I said. "Why?"

"I'm trying to understand you."

"It's that it moved so far. It's that I've never before thought about *life*, if you know what I mean."

"No, I don't," he said.

"Well, what is life and stuff like that."

"Stuff like that. At your age."

I said, "You are much older than I am."

"That still makes you thirty-four and too old for stuff like that."

"You're making fun of me."

"Cut it out, Lilly. I know all the signs."

"Signs of what?"

He got up and left the room. I carried up a martini an hour later and said, "Just this turtle, the next I'll be O.K."

"Fine with me," he said, "either way."

"No, it isn't fine with you. You're saying something else."

"I'm saying cut it out."

"And *I'm* saying — "

"I don't want any dinner," he said.

I left the room and slammed the door. At dinnertime I sent Helen up to tell him to come down immediately and she came back and said he said he wasn't hungry immediately.

During dinner she said she didn't want the turtle around when she came down for breakfast.

About ten, when Helen had gone to bed, I went upstairs and threw a book against Hammett's door.

"Yes?" he said.

"Please come and help me bury the turtle."

"I don't bury turtles."

"Will you bury me?"

"When the times comes, I'll do my best," he said.

"Open the door."

"No. Get Fred Herrmann to help you bury the turtle. And borrow Helen's prayer book."

But by the time I had had three more drinks, it was too late to wake Fred. I went to look at the turtle and saw that its blood was dripping to the floor. For many years, and for many years to come, I had been frightened of Helen and so, toward midnight, I tied a rope around the turtle's tail, took a flashlight, dragged it down the kitchen steps to the garage, and tied the rope to the bumper of the car. Then I went back to stand under Hammett's window.

I shouted up. "I'm weak. I can't dig a hole big enough. Come help me."

After I had said it twice, he called down, "I wish I could help you, but I'm asleep."

I spent the next hour digging a hole on the high ground above the lake, and by the time I covered the turtle the whiskey in the bottle was gone and I was dizzy and feeling sick. I put a stick over the grave, drove the car back towards the house, and when I was halfway there evidently fell asleep because I woke up at dawn in a heavy rain with the right wheels of the car turned into a tree stump. I walked home to bed and neither Hammett nor I mentioned the turtle for four or five days. That was no accident because we didn't speak to each other for three of those days, eating our meals at separate times.

Then he came back from a late afternoon walk and

said, "I've caught two turtles. What would you like
to do with them?"

"Kill them. Make soup."

"You're sure?'

"The first of anything is hard," I said. "You know
that."

"I didn't know that until I met you," he said.

"I hurt my back digging the grave and I've a cold,
but I had to bury that turtle and I don't want to talk
about it again."

"You didn't do it very well. Some animal's been at
your grave and eaten the turtle, but God will bless
you anyway. I gathered the bones, put them back in
the hole, and painted a tombstone sign for you."

For all the years we lived on the place, and maybe
even now, there was a small wooden sign, neatly
painted: "My first turtle is buried here. Miss Religious L.H."

PENTIMENTO

I N 1961, a few weeks after Hammett's death, I moved to Cambridge to teach a writing seminar at Harvard. I had thought Hammett would be coming with me and had arranged with the help of Harry and Elena Levin for a room in a nursing home, a pleasant, sprawling nineteenth century house a few blocks away. Now, living with Helen on the top floor of Leverett Towers, a new student building, I could look down on the nursing home from the window and one night, when I couldn't sleep, I went to stand in front of it. That got to be a habit, and two or three times a week I would walk to the house Hammett had never seen, stand until I was too cold to stand any longer, and go back to bed.

The fifth or sixth time I took my late night walk — Helen was a heavy sleeper and I didn't think there was a chance that I could wake her as I dressed quietly in the next room — there had been a snowstorm during the day that made the few blocks hard going and slippery. But I never reached the nursing home that night, turning back for a reason I didn't as yet know, into Athens Street. Long before I reached our corner I saw Helen, looking very black in her useless summer white raincoat, standing with a tall boy who was holding a motorcycle. I felt the combination of gratitude and resentment I had so often felt for her through the years, but I didn't wish to waste time with it that night.

"Bad night," I said as I went past them.

I heard them behind me as I reached the courtyard of the building, and then I heard a misstep and a sound. As I turned, Helen had slipped, but the boy had caught the great weight and was holding to her, sensibly waiting for her to straighten herself. I knew she would not like me to see this, and so I went on into the building, took one elevator, waited until I heard her take another, heard the boy say something outside our door, and closed my own door against whatever she might say to me.

A few days later I saw her cross the courtyard, the tall boy behind her carrying two large bags of groceries. As she opened our door she took the bags from him and said, "Thank you, son. Come whenever you want your good dinner."

That night I said to her, "You've got a good-looking beau."

She had very little humor, but she liked that kind

288

of simple stuff. Now she didn't answer me and I realized that for the last few days she had said almost nothing to me. She gave me my dinner in silence. After dinner I read for a while, felt restless, and went to get my coat. She came out of her room.

"Death ain't what you think," she said.

"I don't know what it is, do you?"

"A rest. Not for us to understand."

I was used to this palaver, but that night I was ill-humored and made a restless movement.

"I don't want to talk about death."

As I stood waiting for the elevator, she watched me from the doorway.

"You go stand in front of that place because you think you can bring him back. Maybe he don't want to come back, and maybe you don't — " she shrugged, always a sign that she had caught herself at something she considered unwise or useless to continue with.

It was a long time before I knew what she had been about to say, and it was at least a year later, after I had moved back to New York, before I knew that she had discussed me with the tall boy. I thought that was disloyal of her and struggled for months about telling her that, and then knew it wasn't disloyal, and didn't care any more because I had come to like the boy and to understand she had needed him at a lonely time in her own life, in a strange city, living with a woman who did odd things at night.

Soon after the night we had talked about death I

came into the apartment to change my clothes for a dinner with friends. The boy was sitting at the table, Helen opposite him. He got up when I came into the room. We shook hands and Helen said to him, "Sit you down and eat your soufflé before it falls." As I went to my room I heard him say to her, "I never ate a soufflé before. It's wonderful."

"You can have one every night," she said, "a different kind."

When I came out of the bath I could see the boy from the hall mopping the kitchen floor. Helen came into my room.

"He eats nice. Two steaks."

I laughed. *"Two* steaks?"

"He asked what you'd think about that. I told him you got some strange sides, getting stranger, but you don't think about things like that."

"Thank you."

"He is taking me for a drive Thursday."

"On that motorcycle?"

"His rich roommate got a car. He says his roommate's on the stuff."

This then new way of saying dope, the only modern phrase I had ever heard Helen use, was no surprise. Years before she had told me her son was on the stuff and she would have to take him back to South Carolina to the farm her family still owned.

That Thursday, her day off, she got ready early in the morning and looked mighty handsome and big in a suit and a great coat.

"This early?" I said. "Doesn't he go to classes?"

"Jimsie is very, very bright," she said.

"What is Jimsie's last name?"

"I don't know," she said, "he's poor."

Jimsie was not as young as his classmates. He was twenty when we met him in his sophomore year. He told me he had had to wait to save a little money and win a scholarship, and when I asked him what his father did he laughed and said that nobody in his family had earned a living for three generations. He came from Oregon and one night he told funny stories about his mother and father, his five sisters and brothers.

I said, "You like them. That's unusual."

"Like them? I don't know."

"You don't know?"

"I don't know what they mean when they use words like that. I like to be around some people, or my motorcycle, and chemistry. I like one thing more than another. But that's all. Is that bad?"

I said I didn't know, I wasn't that kind of teacher. Then he went back to talking about his family and read me a letter from his father. His father wrote that a doctor in Portland had diagnosed stomach cancer but that he himself had cured it with a mixture of hot beer, cloves, and a sweet onion.

Through that first year I spent at Harvard, Jimsie would drop in at least three or four times a week to see Helen, carry her packages from the market, borrow his roommate's car to take her on small trips.

291

Often he would stay to eat dinner with her and sometimes with me.

It was the period of the early student movement and there was a time when he disappeared into Mississippi and came back beaten up around the kidneys, a favorite place, then and now, for a police beating since it doesn't show. Helen moved him in with us for a week, saying that a roommate who was on the stuff would be no good as a nurse. Jimsie was puzzled, uneasy about the fuss she made over him. And her lack of response to the state of the Negro in the South made him stubborn and nagging. It took years for him to know that it had to do with her age and time: her anger was so great, hidden so deep for so long, that it frightened her and she couldn't face it. He didn't understand her at all, in fact, and there was a funny, nice night in which his attempt to explain to her the reasons for the insanity of the Bay of Pigs was hilarious to hear. She didn't like talk like that: she liked best the times when he played his harmonica, and once she told me with pride that while she had not seen his "report card" another boy in the building had told her he was the most brilliant man in the class who played a harmonica.

In May of that year, about a week before we were to leave Cambridge, I woke up, knocked over an ashtray, and lay sweating with the mess I had been dreaming. After a while I got up, put on a coat and walked to the nursing home, certain that I would never go again. I stood in front of it for a long time, and when I turned to go back, Jimsie was directly behind me. I knew, of course, that Helen had telephoned him, but now, as we walked together, I had no concern for either of them. We didn't speak until I heard myself say, "Pentimento."

"What's that mean?" he said.

I said, "Don't follow me again, Jimsie, I don't like it."

But I don't wish to write about Jimsie; that isn't the point here and he wouldn't like it. Everybody else in this book is dead. We have become good friends, although now, twelve years after I met him, I don't understand him, or why he has decided on a life so different from the one he planned the year I met him. He was a chemistry student then and stayed on, after graduation, to work with Robert Woodward, the Nobel laureate, and spoke of the beauties and mysteries of chemistry with an emotion he showed for nothing else. Then he suddenly switched to astrophysics, and the night he tried to tell Helen what that meant she said he gave her a headache for a week, and because she came down with a bad cold after the headache and died from pneumonia a month later, I have always thought of astrophysics as having to do with her last days.

Jimsie was at the funeral in the ugly Harlem funeral place and I saw him standing in the rear, talking to her son. But by the time I reached the back of the place, through the mass of incompetent relatives she had been supporting for years, he had disappeared, and it was only last year that I found out it was he, not her son, who had taken the coffin by train to Camden, South Carolina, and waited with it on the station platform for a night and a day until her sister and brothers came a long distance over country roads to take it from him.

Somewhere in the years before or after that, I can no longer remember, Jimsie won a Marshall Scholarship, harder to earn than a Rhodes or a Fulbright, and went off to study in Cambridge, England. A friend of mine, an old Cambridge graduate, sent me a letter: "He has dazzled them here. I took him out for a drink, less because you wrote than because he is so interesting. But something has gone awry: I don't think he wants astrophysics, I think the world puzzles him."

I guess that was true, because he returned to Harvard, although I am no longer clear about when or why, except that he was there when I went back to teach in 1968, the year of the student riots. I remember that one day, at the height of the protests, we walked together in the Harvard Yard. George Wald, who had been a hero, and may be again, was not doing well that day as he stood before students making a conciliatory speech, too sure that his audience was with him, he with them. There were angry boos and the boy in front of us took an apple from his pocket and raised his arm for the pitch. Jimsie caught his arm and said, "Put it down, kiddie, a fine way of saying no to an old man." The boy pulled away angrily until he turned and recognized Jimsie, and then he said, "Oh, it's you," and patted him on the shoulder.

I guess he went back to England, because sometime in 1970 I had a short letter: "Do you think I can write? Of course not. But I'm through with astrophysics. I don't intend to work for the bastards and there is no other place to take it." I wrote back to say I didn't think he should try writing and didn't hear again until I had a card with an Albanian postmark that says, "I like these folks. They're willing to fight everybody and they know the reason why. See you soon."

But it wasn't soon, not until last year during the summer, when I had a letter from Oregon saying he was back there, his father had given him forty acres of ruined land, the way everything his family touched was ruined, things were agreeable, but he was sick of communal life except for Carrie, who was clean and hard-working. A few days before this Christmas he called me, said he was in New York, could he take me to dinner?

It was good to see him again. The too bony face and body had grown now into power and full masculine good looks. We ate in a Greenwich Village fancy joint one of his friends had told him about and he whistled when he saw the prices on the menu.

He said, "I can't buy you dinner. I thought I could, but I can't at these prices."

"I'll buy it for you. It doesn't matter."

"Yes, it does, but never mind. You look tired. Is something wrong?"

"I am tired."

"Come to Oregon. I'll take care of you. Carrie has learned to cook and she scrubs around. I can't stand dirt. My mother is such a slob. A pretty, nice lady, but a slob."

"You like Carrie?"

"She's O.K."

"That's all?"

"Isn't that enough?"

"No," I said, "I don't think so."

"Not for you," he said. "For me."

"Do you farm the land?"

He laughed. "I have a good vegetable garden and I had a hundred chickens, but my father killed the chickens for a neighborhood celebration. I earn a living as a carpenter and now, *now*, I'm getting rich. Some ass in Portland, a woman decorator, sells what she calls rosettes des bois and I carve them for her. Got that? I make *rosettes des bois.*"

"Somewhere I know those words," I said, "but I can't remember —"

"They're rosettes of wood and you stick them on headboards of beds or old armoires, mostly new junk you fix to make old. She started out paying me five bucks apiece but now she pays me twenty-five. I'll get more when I get around to telling her I want it. Good?"

When I didn't answer, he put down his fork. "Good?"

"Stop it," I said. "You know what I think. Do you want another steak?"

He laughed. "If you've got the money, yes. Helen told you about the two steaks she used to cook me?"

"Yes."

"That great, big, fine lady, doing her best in this world. Do you know she gave me this coat?" He pointed to a sheepskin coat, expensive but old, lying on the chair next to him. "And when I brought it to her, said it cost too much, couldn't take presents from a working lady, know what she did? She slapped my face."

"You once told me you didn't understand about like or dislike."

He said, "I loved Helen."

"Too bad you never told her so. Too late now."

"I told it to her," he said, "the night I looked up your word, pentimento."